READY TO READ MUSIC

SEQUENTIAL LESSONS IN MUSIC READING
Jay Althouse

Alfred Music
P.O. Box 10003
Van Nuys, CA 91410-0003
alfred.com

ISBN-10: 0-7390-3285-2 (Book)
ISBN-13: 978-0-7390-3285-5 (Book)

ISBN-10: 0-7390-9670-2 (Book & Data CD)
ISBN-13: 978-0-7390-9670-3 (Book & Data CD)

WHEN YOUR STUDENTS ARE "READY TO READ MUSIC..."

Discover Alfred's popular "READY TO SING" Songbook Series

Compiled and Edited by Jay Althouse

This exciting "ready-to-use" songbook series features favorite songs arranged for voice and piano in a simple style—appropriate for beginning and young soloists, unison classroom singing, and elementary choral groups. Each book includes reproducible melody line song sheets which can be distributed to singers. Easy piano accompaniments double or strongly support the melody throughout each song. Vocal ranges are moderate; most have a one-octave range.

- Recommended for grades 2–8.
- Reproducible Student Song Sheets included.

Ready to Sing... Christmas

13 Christmas Favorites, Simply Arranged for Voice and Piano, for Solo or Unison Singing

13 holiday favorites, great for holiday sing-alongs! Includes:

- A-Rockin' All Night
- Away in a Manger
- Deck the Hall
- Ding Dong! Merrily on High
- The First Noel
- Frozen December
- Fum, Fum, Fum
- Good King Wenceslas
- Jingle Bells
- Joy to the World
- Over the River and Through the Wood
- Silent Night
- Still, Still, Still

Book 20195
Book/Accompaniment CD 20197

Ready to Sing... Folk Songs

10 Folk Songs, Simply Arranged for Voice and Piano, for Solo or Unison Singing

This excellent collection of 10 folk songs includes three with optional non-English texts, but English may be sung throughout. Includes:

- All Through the Night
- Li'l Liza Jane
- Siyahamba
- Scarborough Fair
- Skye Boat Song
- The Water Is Wide
- Ma Bella Bimba
- Oh, Susanna
- Poor Wayfaring Stranger
- De Colores

Book 17173
Book/Accompaniment CD 17175

Ready to Sing... Spirituals

11 Spirituals, Simply Arranged for Voice and Piano, for Solo or Unison Singing

A wonderful variety of 11 favorite spirituals. Includes:

- Gospel Train
- Ride the Chariot
- Kum Ba Yah
- Down by the Riverside
- Wade in the Water
- Yes, My Lord!
- Amazing Grace
- Go, Tell It on the Mountain
- Joshua
- Good News!
- Nobody Knows the Trouble I've Seen

Book 19809
Book/Accompaniment CD 19811

INTRODUCTION

Too often, students are unprepared when printed music is placed in front of them. The goal of *Ready to Read Music* is to prepare students for their first encounter with printed music.

Ready to Read Music is based on the principle of readiness as a preparation for the study of a skill. For example, before a student can read words and sentences, he or she must learn the letters of the alphabet and the sounds of the English language. Then and only then is the student ready to read words.

We've taken the same approach with this book. Music, like any language, is comprised of a limited number of symbols. Learn the symbols and you can learn the language. The period during which the student learns the symbols of music is a transition period in which the student gradually becomes prepared to read music. In a series of four sequential units of eight lessons each, the student is introduced to the fundamental symbols of music. By the end of this book, the student will be able to identify these symbols and elements of music and is, indeed, *Ready to Read Music*.

How to Use This Book

Ready to Read Music consists of four units of eight lessons each. Both the units and the lessons are sequential; each unit and lesson builds on what the student has learned in previous units and lessons. Most of the lessons are one page in length (though a few are two) and introduce one musical symbol or concept. A one-page review follows most, but not all of the lessons.

This book is 100% reproducible. You may photocopy and distribute every page to your students. Students may assemble the lessons into a notebook. Review pages may be used as an assessment tool for each lesson.

Throughout the book, notes and other musical symbols are always shown as they would be used in a piece of music; i.e., on the staff. Attention is paid to the correct positioning of notes and other symbols on the staff. This helps to establish good student notational skills, essential in several of the National Standards for Music Education. These include Content Standard 4, "composing and arranging music within specified guidelines," and Content Standard 5, "reading and notating music."

The four units are as follows:

Unit 1 introduces the musical staff, the treble and bass clef, and the following notes: whole note, half note, quarter note, and eighth note. Students are asked to draw and identify the clefs and notes. The duration of the various notes is introduced by relating them to mathematics with a graph/chart in Unit 1, Lesson 4.

Unit 2 focuses on the concept of rhythm by introducing rests for each of the notes introduced in Unit 1, measures, barlines, and the concept of beat. Also introduced are time signatures, dotted notes and rests, and tied notes.

Unit 3 introduces pitch. Students learn the letter names for notes in both clefs including three ledger lines. The two clefs are combined into the grand staff in Lesson 5. Sharps, flats, and key signatures follow, along with the natural sign.

Unit 4 introduces more musical symbols and terms including those which indicate how loud (or how soft) and how fast (or how slowly) music should be performed. Also included in Unit 4 are the staccato dot, the fermata, accents, repeat signs, and first and second endings. Lesson 7 introduces a vocal staff above a piano accompaniment. Lesson 8, "Putting It All Together," is a two page piece of music in which every musical symbol is identified.

The student is now *Ready to Read Music*. A full-length, four page musical work, an arrangement of the folk song, *The Water Is Wide*, is included on page 116. This piece may be photocopied and distributed to students as the first piece of music which they truly read.

Beginning on page 75 are full size, reproducible pages of each of the musical symbols or terms used in this book. They are shown in the order in which they were introduced. These pages may be used on bulletin boards or may be reproduced and distributed to students as part of their lessons. As in the book, the symbols are always shown as they would be used in a piece of music.

Answer keys for the student review pages are on pages 110-115. A reproducible certificate, to be signed by the teacher and distributed to students who complete the book, is shown on page 120.

ABOUT THE AUTHOR

Jay Althouse received a B.S. degree in Music Education and an M.Ed. degree in Music from Indiana University of Pennsylvania. For eight years he served as a rights and licenses administrator for a major educational music publisher. During that time he served a term on the Executive Board of the Music Publishers Association of America.

As a composer of sacred and secular choral music, Mr. Althouse has over 500 works in print for choirs of all levels.

His music is widely performed throughout the English-speaking world. He is a writer member of ASCAP and is a regular recipient of the ASCAP Special Award for his compositions in the area of standard music.

His book, *Copyright: The Complete Guide for Music Educators* has been in print continuously since 1984 and is recognized as the definitive sourcebook on the subject of copyright for music educators. An updated, second edition was released in 1999.

Mr. Althouse has also co-written several cantatas and musicals with his wife, Sally K. Albrecht, compiled and arranged a number of highly regarded vocal solo collections, and is the co-writer of the best-selling book, *The Complete Choral Warm-up Book*, published by Alfred Music. Most recently, he co-authored *Accent on Composers*, a reproducible sourcebook for classroom music teachers featuring the music and lives of 22 composers.

Unit 1
Staff, Clefs, Notes

LESSON 1 *The Staff*

Before you learned to read, you learned the letters of the alphabet. Letters are the symbols that make up words.

Learning to read music is the same. Before you can read music you must learn the symbols of music. Just as the letters of the alphabet can be combined to form words and sentences, the symbols of music can be combined to form music. When you have learned the symbols of music, you will see how they are combined to form music.

The symbols of music are music are placed on, or between, or near a group of five lines and four spaces called a **staff**. A **staff** usually runs all the way across a page, like this:

The lines of a **staff** and the spaces between the lines are numbered, like this:

5th line →
4th line →
3rd line →
2nd line →
1st line →
← 4th space
← 3rd space
← 2nd space
← 1st space

Write an x on the correct line, or in the correct space.

| Write an x on the 3rd line | Write an x in the 4th space | Write an x on the 1st line | Write an x in the 2nd space | Write an x on the 3rd line |

The x is on which line or in which space?

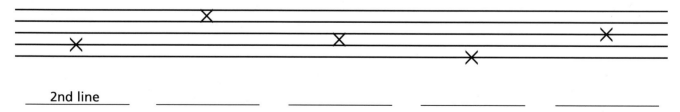

2nd line

LESSON 2 *Treble Clef*

Just as we read words and sentences from left to right,
we read the symbols of music from left to right on a **staff**.

The first musical symbol placed at
the left of a **staff** is called a **clef sign**.
This **clef sign** is called a **treble clef**
(pronounced TREH-bul clef).

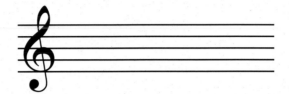

The **treble clef** is also known as the **G clef.**

Here's how to draw a
treble clef on a **staff**.

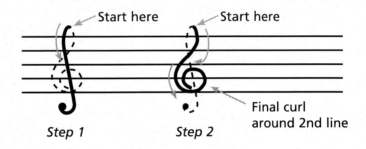

Start here   Start here

Final curl
around 2nd line

Step 1   *Step 2*

Trace the first **treble clef**, then draw five more **treble clefs** to the right of the first one.

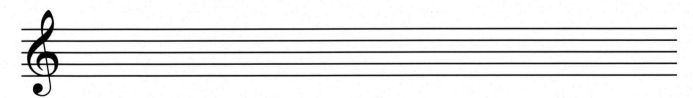

LESSON 3 | *Bass Clef*

Another **clef sign** which can be placed
at the beginning of the **staff** is called the
bass clef (pronounced the same as the
word "base"). The **bass clef** looks like this.

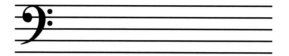

The **bass clef** is also known as the **F clef.**

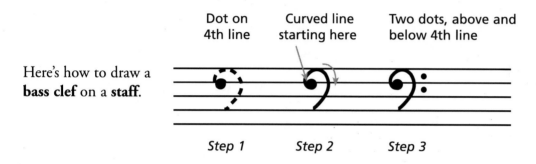

| Dot on | Curved line | Two dots, above and |
| 4th line | starting here | below 4th line |

Here's how to draw a
bass clef on a **staff**.

Step 1   *Step 2*   *Step 3*

The starting dot goes on the 4th line.
The two finishing dots go above and below the 4th line.

Trace the first **bass clef**, then draw five more **bass clefs** to the right of the first one.

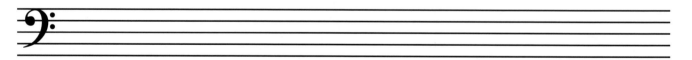

LESSON 4 *Notes*

The most important musical symbols placed on a **staff** are called **notes**.
The four most common **notes** are:

Whole note   **Half note**

Quarter note   **Eighth note**

Notes tell us several things. One of the things a **note** tells us is how long to sing or play a sound.
Some **notes** last for a long time and some for a short time.
Of the four **notes** shown above, a **whole note** is the longest and an **eighth note** is the shortest.
It's a little bit like arithmetic.

MusicMath

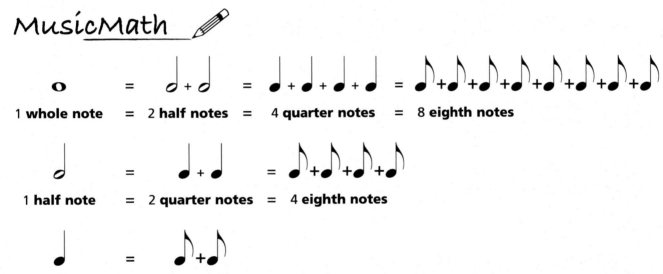

1 **whole note**   =   2 **half notes**   =   4 **quarter notes**   =   8 **eighth notes**

1 **half note**   =   2 **quarter notes**   =   4 **eighth notes**

1 **quarter note**   =   2 **eighth notes**.

Here's another way of showing the length of these **notes**:

LESSON 5 *Whole Note*

This is a **whole note**. A **whole note** is the longest note we learned in the last lesson.

The **whole note** is the easiest to draw. Just draw an oval, like this.

Trace the **whole note** shown below. Then draw five **whole notes** to the right of the **note** you traced.

Whole notes look like this on a **staff**:

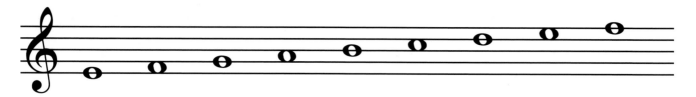

When a **whole note** is in a space, it fills the space from top to bottom, like this:

When it's on a line, it is centered on the line, like this:

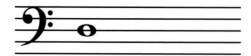

Trace the first **whole note** below. Then draw five more **whole notes** anywhere on the **staff**.

LESSON 5
REVIEW
Whole Note

Circle all the **whole notes** in the staff below.

Draw a **whole note** on the line or in the space shown below.

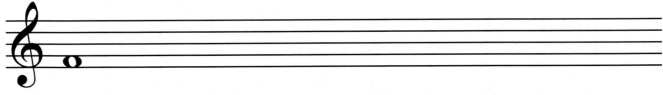

In the 1st space   On the 3rd line   In the 2nd space   On the 5th line   In the 4th space

On which line or in which space have these **whole notes** been placed?

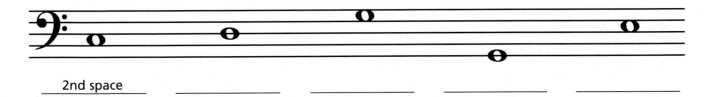

2nd space   _____   _____   _____   _____

Are these **whole notes** in the **treble clef** or the **bass clef**? Circle the correct answer.

A. Treble clef   **B. Bass clef**

LESSON 6   *Half Note*

A **half note** looks like this:

Two **half notes** equal one **whole note**.
A **half note** lasts half as long as a **whole note**.

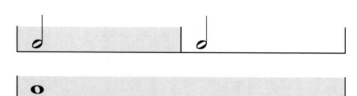

To draw a **half note**, begin by drawing an oval, like a **whole note**. This part of the **note** is called the **notehead**.

Step 1

Then add a line on the right side of the **notehead**, like this. The line is called a **stem**.

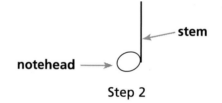

notehead →

Step 2

Sometimes the **stem** goes down, like this. If the **stem** goes down, it's on the left side of the **notehead**. If the **stem** goes up, it's on the right side of the **notehead**.

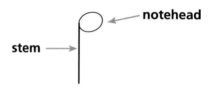

Trace each **half note** shown below. Then draw three more **half notes** to the right of each one you traced.

Half notes look like this on a **staff**:

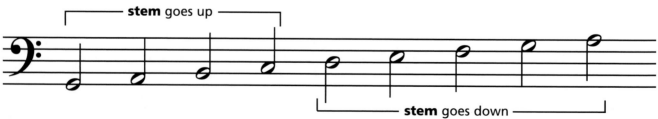

All **half notes** below the 3rd line have the **stem** going up.
All **half notes** on or above the 3rd line have the **stem** going down.

LESSON 6
REVIEW *Half Note*

Draw a **half note** on the line or in the space shown below. Make sure the **stems** go in the correct direction.

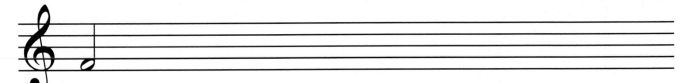

In the 1st space   On the 4th line   In the 3rd space   On the 2nd line   On the 5th line

On which line or in which space have these **half notes** been placed?

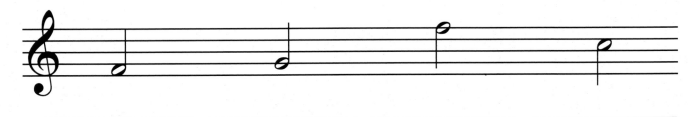

_____   _____   _____   _____

Are these **half notes** in the **treble clef** or the **bass clef**? Circle the correct answer.

A. Treble clef   **B. Bass clef**

MusicMath

In each of the pairs of examples below, one example is correct and one is incorrect.
Circle each example that is correct.

1. A. 𝅗𝅥 + 𝅗𝅥 = 𝅝   OR   B. 𝅝 + 𝅝 = 𝅗𝅥

 2. A. ⟨staff example⟩   OR   B.

LESSON 7 *Quarter Note*

A **quarter note** looks like this:

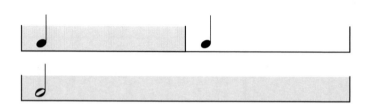

Two **quarter notes** equal one **half note.**
A **quarter note** lasts half as long as a **half note.**

To draw a **quarter note**, begin by drawing
an oval, which is the **notehead**.

Step 1

Now, fill in the **notehead**, then add a **stem.**

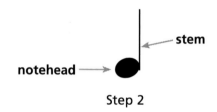

Step 2

Sometimes the **stem** goes down,
just like on a **half note.**

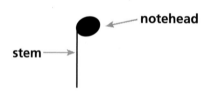

Trace each **quarter note** shown below. Then draw three more **quarter notes** to the right of each one you traced.

Quarter notes look like this on a **staff**:

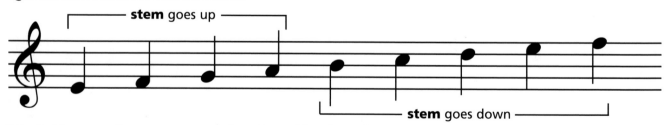

Like **half notes**, all **quarter notes** below the 3rd line have the **stem** going up.
All **quarter notes** on or above the 3rd line have the **stem** going down.

LESSON 7 — *Quarter Note*
REVIEW

Draw a **quarter note** on the line or in the space shown below. Make sure the **stems** go in the correct direction.

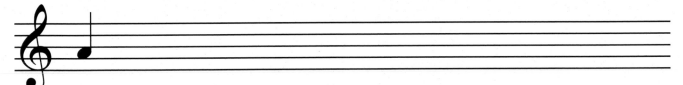

In the 2nd space   On the 2nd line   On the 3rd line   On the 5th line   In the 3rd space

On which line or in which space have these **quarter notes** been placed?

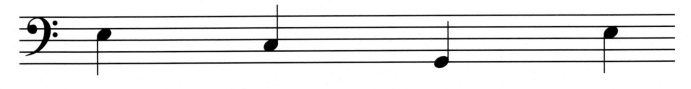

Are there more **quarter notes** or **half notes** on this **staff**? Circle the correct answer.

A. More **quarter notes**   **B.** More **half notes**

MusicMath

Circle the example that is correct.

A. ♩ + ♩ = ♩   OR   **B.** ♩ + ♩ = ♪

True or false? Circle the correct answer for each.

♪ + ♪ = o   True   False

♩ + ♩ = ♪   True   False

LESSON 8 *Eighth Note*

An **eighth note** looks like this:

Two **eighth notes** equal one **quarter note**.
An **eighth note** lasts half as long as a **quarter note**.

To draw an **eighth note**, begin by drawing a **quarter note**.

Step 1

Then add a curved line to the top of the **stem**, like this. This curved line is called a **flag**. (It looks a little like a flag hanging on a flagpole, don't you think?)

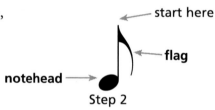

start here

flag

notehead →

Step 2

Sometimes, like **half notes and quarter notes**, the **stem** goes down.

Notice the **stem** is now on the left, but the **flag** is still on the right side of the **stem**.

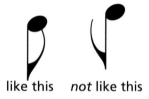

like this   *not* like this

Trace each **eighth note** shown below. Then draw three more **eighth notes** to the right of each one you traced.

Eighth notes look like this on a **staff**.

stem goes up

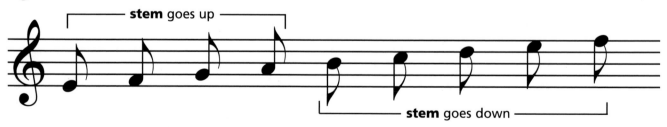

stem goes down

Like **half notes** and **quarter notes**, all **eighth notes** below the 3rd line have the **stem** going up.
All **eighth notes** on or above the 3rd line have the **stem** going down.

LESSON 8
REVIEW   *Eighth Note*

Draw an **eighth note** on the line or in the space shown below. Make sure the **stems** go in the correct direction.

In the 4th space   On the 3rd line   On the 1st line   On the 2nd line   In the 3rd space

On which line or in which space have these **eighth notes** been placed?

_____   _____   _____   _____

Sometimes, two, three, or four **eighth notes** are written together like this.

beam

The line that connects the **eighth notes** is called a **beam.**

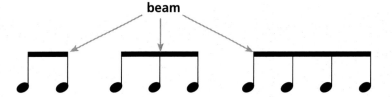

Add the **stems** to these **eighth notes** and connect them with a **beam.**
Make sure the **stems** go in the correct direction.

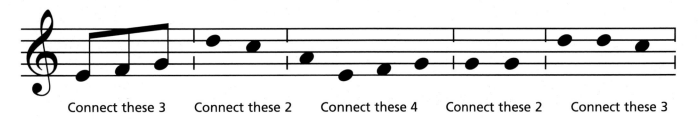

Connect these 3   Connect these 2   Connect these 4   Connect these 2   Connect these 3

UNIT 2
Rhythm

LESSON 1   *Rests*

Music is more than just one **note** or musical sound after another. Sometimes there is silence in the music. The musical symbol for silence is called a **rest**. For every type of note (**whole note**, **half note**, **quarter note**, **eighth note**) there is a **rest**.

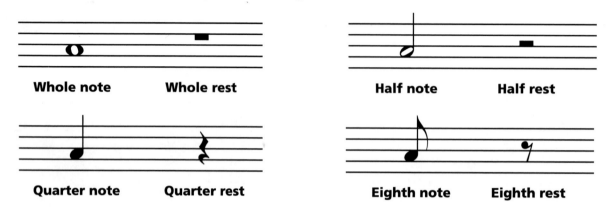

Whole note   **Whole rest**   **Half note**   **Half rest**

Quarter note   **Quarter rest**   **Eighth note**   **Eighth rest**

MusicMath

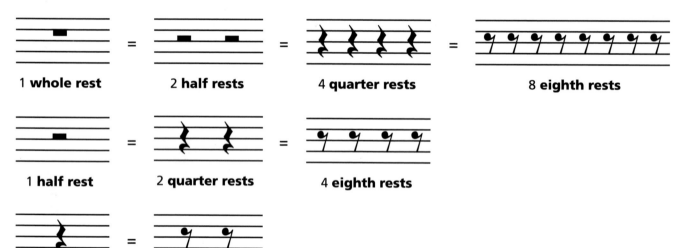

1 **whole rest**   2 **half rests**   4 **quarter rests**   8 **eighth rests**

1 **half rest**   2 **quarter rests**   4 **eighth rests**

1 **quarter rest**   2 **eighth rests**

Here's another way of showing the length of these **rests**:

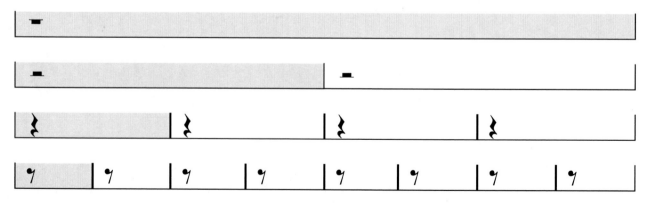

REVIEW *Rests*

Circle all the **whole rests** on this **staff**.

Circle all the **half rests** on this **staff**.

Circle all the **quarter rests** on this **staff**.

Circle all the **eighth rests** on this **staff**.

MusicMath ✏

Write T if the MusicMath is True. Write F if the MusicMath is False.

1. _____   T

2. _____

3. _____

4. _____

5. _____

6. _____

LESSON 2   *Whole Rest and Half Rest*

This is a **whole rest**. The silence of a **whole rest** lasts as long as the sound of a **whole note**.

1 **whole rest**   =   1 **whole note**

This is a **half rest**. The silence of a **half rest** lasts as long as the sound of a **half note**.

1 **half rest**   =   1 **half note**

Here's how to draw a **whole rest** and a **half rest**.
They look the same, but they're not. If you look closely, you'll see that. . .

A **whole rest** always "hangs" from the fourth line.

A **half rest** always "sits" on the third line.

Some people remember the difference beteween a **whole rest** and a **half rest** this way: because a **whole rest** lasts longer than a **half rest**, it is "heavier." So it has to "hang" from a line. Because a **half rest** is shorter, it is "lighter," and can "sit" on a line.

Trace the **whole rest** shown below. Then draw five more **whole rests** to the right of the **rest** you traced.

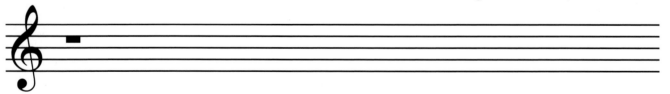

Trace the **half rest** shown below. Then draw five more **half rests** to the right of the **rest** you traced.

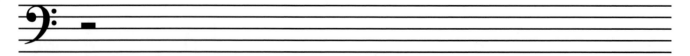

LESSON 2
REVIEW *Whole Rest and Half Rest*

Circle all the **whole rests** in the **staff** below.

Circle all the **half rests** in the **staff** below.

Only one of the **rests** below is a correct **whole rest**. Circle it.

Only one of the **rests** below is a correct **half rest**. Circle it.

Whole rest or **half rest** or neither? Circle the correct answer.

Whole rest	Whole rest	Whole rest	Whole rest	Whole rest
Half rest	Half rest	Half rest	Half rest	Half rest
(Neither)	Neither	Neither	Neither	Neither

LESSON 3 — *Quarter Rest and Eighth Rest*

This is a **quarter rest**. The silence of a **quarter rest** lasts as long as the sound of a **quarter note**.

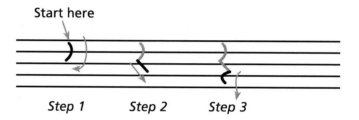

1 **quarter rest**   =   1 **quarter note**

This is an **eighth rest**. The silence of an **eighth rest** lasts as long as the sound of an **eighth note**.

1 **eighth rest**   =   1 **eighth note**

A **quarter rest** is drawn in three steps, like this:

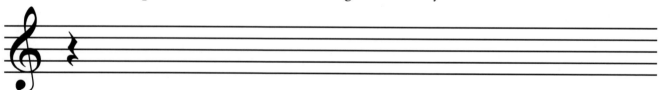

Start here

Step 1   *Step 2*   *Step 3*

Trace the **quarter rest** shown below.
Then draw five more **quarter rests** on the **staff** to the right of the rest you traced.

An **eighth rest** is drawn in two steps, like this:

Start here

Step 1   *Step 2*

Trace the **eighth rest** shown below.
Then draw five more **eighth rests** on the **staff** to the right of the **rest** you traced.

LESSON 3
REVIEW
Quarter Rest and Eighth Rest

Circle all the **quarter rests** in the **staff** below.

Circle all the **eighth rests** in the **staff** below.

What kind of **rests** are shown below? Circle the correct answer.

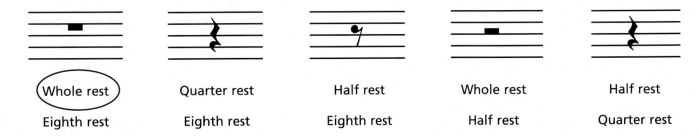

Whole rest   Quarter rest   Half rest   Whole rest   Half rest

Eighth rest   Eighth rest   Eighth rest   Half rest   Quarter rest

MusicMath

True or false? Circle the correct answer for each.

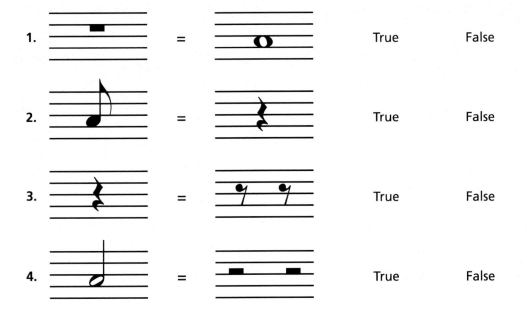

1.   =　True　False

2.   =　True　False

3.   =　True　False

4.   =　True　False

LESSON 4 *Barlines and Measures*

Look at the **notes** on this **staff**.

Suppose your teacher asked you to play this **note**. She would have to say, "Play the tenth **note** on the **staff**," and you would have to count from left to right until you found it.

Notes are easier to read on a **staff** when they are divided into groups.
Notes are divided into groups with lines called **barlines**, like this:

The groups of **notes** between the **barlines** are called **measures**.
(They can also be called **bars**, but we'll call them **measures**.)

Now your teacher can say, "Play the second **note** in
the third **measure**," and you can find it more quickly.

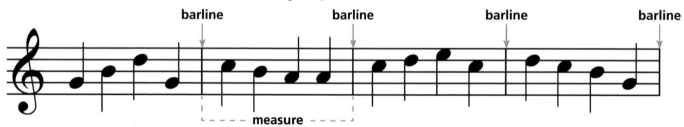

MUSICAL RULE — There is always a **barline** at the end of every **staff.**

Put a **barline** after every fourth **note**.

Put a **barline** after every third **note**.

LESSON 4 REVIEW — *Barlines and Measures*

Circle the second **note** in the second **measure** and the third **note** in the fourth **measure**.

Rests can be written in place of **notes** in a **measure**, like this.
Circle every **half note** and every **half rest** in this example.

Put three **quarter notes** and one one **quarter rest** in each **measure**,
using the instructions below the staff. Place the **quarter notes** anywhere on the **staff**, some on **lines** and some in **spaces**.

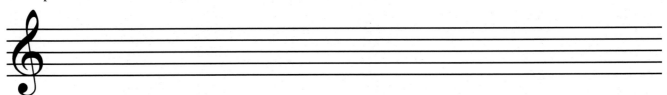

    note   note   note   rest   note   rest   note   note   rest   note   note   note

Using **barlines**, divide the **staff** below into four **measures**.
Then place one **half note** and one **half rest** in each **measure**.

MusicMath ✐

The first **measure** has a **whole note**. The second **measure** has two
half notes. Place four **notes** in the third **measure** that equal the
value of the **notes** in the first two **measures**.

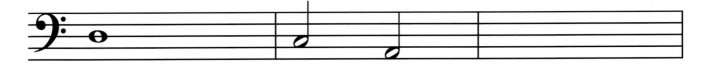

What kind of **note** did you
place in the third **measure**? _____

LESSON 5 *Beats*

Do you know how to feel your heartbeat? Place the first two fingers of either hand
on the left or right front of your neck and you will feel your heartbeat. This steady
heartbeat is also called your pulse. Each pulse of your heart is called a beat.

Music has a steady pulse, too. Just like your heart, each pulse of music is called a **beat**.

Tap your fingers on your desk with a steady **beat**. Follow the **notes** below with each tap.
Each **quarter note** gets one tap of your fingers. On this **staff** each **quarter note** gets one **beat**.

Now tap it again, but this time, tap a little louder on the first **note** in each **measure**.

In the example above, there are four **quarter note beats** in each **measure**. **Half notes** and **eighth notes** can be used as a **beat**, too.

There are three **half note beats** in these **measures**.

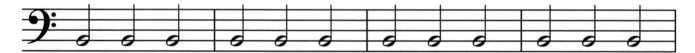

There are six **eighth note beats** in these **measures**.

Rests can be **beats**, too. Tap each of these **notes**, but don't tap the **rests**.
Feel the pulse of the **beat** for the **rest**, but don't tap it.

LESSON 5 *Beats*
REVIEW

If a **quarter note** gets one **beat**, how
many **beats** are there in this **measure**?

_____

If a **half note** gets one **beat**, how
many **beats** are in this **measure**?

_____

If an **eighth note** gets one **beat**, how
many **beats** are in this **measure**?

_____

In the **staff** below, a **quarter note** gets one **beat**.
Place **barlines** after every three **beats**.

In the **staff** below, a **quarter note** gets one **beat**.
Place **barlines** after every four **beats**.

LESSON 6 *Time Signature*

How do music readers know how many **beats** there are in a **measure**? They know because at the beginning of a piece of music, to the right of the **clef** sign, are two numbers, one above the other, like this:

These two numbers are called a **time signature**.
(It's also called a **meter signature**, but we'll call it a **time signature**.)

The top number of the **time signature** tells us how many **beats** there are in each **measure**.

The bottom number of the **time signature** tells us which **note** gets one **beat**.
Here's how to know which **note** gets one **beat**:

- if the bottom number is a 2, a **half note** gets one **beat**.
- if the bottom number is a 4, a **quarter note** gets one **beat**.
- if the bottom number is an 8, an **eighth note** gets one **beat**.

 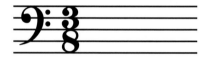 

This **time signature** is four-four. There are four **beats** in each **measure** and a **quarter note** gets one **beat**.

This **time signature** is three-eight. There are three **beats** in each **measure** and an **eighth note** gets one **beat**.

This **time signature** is two-two. There are two **beats** in each **measure** and a **half note** gets one **beat**.

Circle the **note** which gets one **beat** in each of the following examples.

LESSON 6 REVIEW   *Time Signature*

The last **note** is missing in each **measure**. Write one **note** in each box to complete each **measure**. Put the **note** on any **line** or in any **space**. (Remember, the **time signature** will tell you how many **beats** are in each **measure**, and what **note** gets a **beat**.)

Write one **rest** in each box to complete each **measure**.

On the **staff** below, one **measure** has too many **beats**. Circle the **measure** with too many **beats**.

On the **staff** below, one **measure** doesn't have enough **beats**. Circle that **measure**.

Write the correct **time signature** in the box for each of the following examples.

LESSON 7 *Dots*

The fourth **measure** in this musical example in three-four **time signature** is blank. Suppose we wanted to sing one **note** for the three **beats** in the **measure**. What **note** would we put there? A **quarter note** gets one **beat** and a **half note** gets two **beats**. But there is no **note** which gets three **beats**. What do we do?

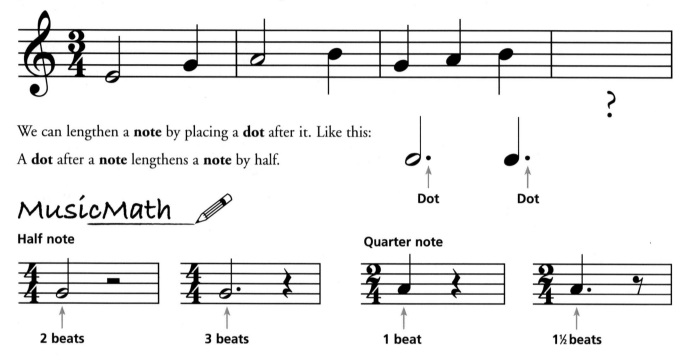

We can lengthen a **note** by placing a **dot** after it. Like this:

A **dot** after a **note** lengthens a **note** by half.

Dot   Dot

MusicMath

Half note

Quarter note

2 beats	3 beats

1 beat	1½ beats

Whole notes and **eighth notes** can also be **dotted**.
However, **dotted half notes** and **dotted quarter notes** are more common.

So we can fill the fourth **measure** of the example at the top of the page with a **dotted half note**. Like this:

Dotted half note

Here are some other examples of music using **dotted notes**.

Rests can be dotted, too, ... like this:

LESSON 7   REVIEW   *Dots*

MusicMath ✏

Write the correct **note** in each blank space.

Fill in the correct **dotted note** in the box.

Fill in the correct **dotted rest** in the box.

Place **barlines** in the correct places on this **staff**.

In the **staff** below, circle the **measure** which has too many **beats**.

LESSON 8 | *Ties*

Suppose we wanted to play one **note** here that lasts for two **beats**.

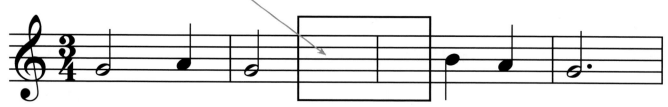

A **half note** gets two **beats**, so could we put a **half note** here?

No, because then there would be too many **beats** in **measure** 2. The **time signature** tells us there must be three **beats** in each **measure**, and now **measure** 2 has four **beats**.

We can solve this by adding a **note** with a curved line called a **tie**. In the last lesson, we learned how to lengthen a **note** by adding a **dot**. We can also lengthen a **note** by **tying** it to another **note** on the same line or in the same space, like this:

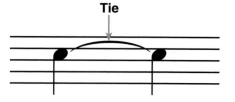

So here's how to play or sing a **note** for two **beats** at the end of **measure** 2. We add a **quarter note** which is **tied** to the **quarter note** in the at the beginning of **measure** 3.

The **quarter note** in **measure** 2 gets one **beat**, and the **quarter note** in **measure** 3 gets one **beat**. When we **tie** these two **quarter notes** together, they sound for two **beats**, the same as a **half note**.

MUSICAL RULE — Two **notes** which are **tied** must be on the same line or in the same space. **Ties** can cross **barlines**. **Ties** go the opposite direction from a **note's** stem.

Like this. . .   . . .*not* like this.   Like this. . .   . . .*not* like this.

LESSON 8 *Ties*
REVIEW

MusicMath

To figure out the value of two **tied notes**, add the value of both **notes**.

There are only two pairs of **notes** in this example which can be **tied**.
Add **ties** to those two pairs of **notes**.

MusicMath

Write the **note** or **dotted note** that equals the **tied notes**.

1. ♩. ⌣ ♩ = _____   3. ♪ ⌣ ♪ = _____

2. ♩. ⌣ ♪ = _____   4. ♩ ⌣ ♩ = _____

Add the correct **note** or **dotted note** to the **tied note**.

1. ♩ = ♩. ⌣ _____   3. ♩ = ♩ ⌣ _____

2. ♩ = ♩ ⌣ _____   4. 𝅝 = ♩ ⌣ _____

UNIT 3
Pitch

LESSON 1 — *Note Names in the Treble Clef*

In Units 1 and 2, we learned how to place **notes** on a **staff**. Look at these **quarter notes** in the **treble clef**.

Suppose we wanted to give names to these **notes** according to their position on the **staff**. We would have to say, "a **note** on the 2nd line, a **note** on the 3rd line, a note in the 3rd space," and so on.

That's a lot of words! Fortunately, there's an easier way to describe or identify **notes**. Each line and space of the **staff** has a name. A letter of the alphabet is used to identify each line or space. Only the first seven letters, A through G, are used. After G, the letters repeat, like this: A, B, C, D, E, F, G, then the letters begin again with A, B, C, and so forth.

The **clef** sign on a **staff** tells us where to place the letter names for the **notes**. Do you remember that the **treble clef** is also known as the **G clef**? Here's why: the final loop of the **treble clef**, around the 2nd line, tells us that the second line is a G.

Here is G in the **treble clef**:

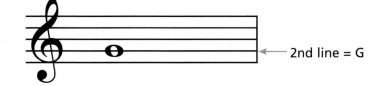

← 2nd line = G

If we know where to find G in the **treble clef**, we can find every other note in the **staff**. Remember: after G, we start the alphabet over again with A. Going up:

G   A   B   C   D   E   F   G

Notice that the space above the top line has a letter name.

Going down, we'll have to go backwards in the alphabet from G, like this:

G   F   E   D

Notice that the space below the bottom line has a letter name.

LESSON 1 *Note Names in the Treble Clef*

Here are all the letter names of the lines and spaces in the **treble clef**.

D E F G A B C D E F G

The spaces, from bottom to top are F-A-C-E. Some people remember this because it spells the word "*face.*"

The lines, from bottom to top are E-G-B-D-F. Some people remember these because it is the first letter from each word in the sentence, "*Every good boy does fine.*"

In Unit 1, we learned that **notes** tell us how long to sing or play a musical sound. **Notes** also tell us how high or how low to sing or play a musical sound. **Notes** which are higher in the **staff** sound higher than **notes** which are lower in the **staff**.

This **note** sounds higher  than this **note**.

Draw a **note** in the box which is lower than the printed **note**.

After the printed **note**, draw three different **notes** which are higher than the printed **note**.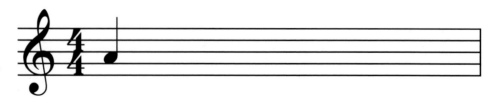

LESSON 1
REVIEW *Note Names in the Treble Clef*

Place the correct letter name under each **note** in the **treble clef**.

C _____ _____ _____ _____ _____ _____

Draw **quarter notes** in the **treble clef** for each of the following letter names. Don't forget to draw the **stem** correctly. (In some cases there may be more than one correct answer.)

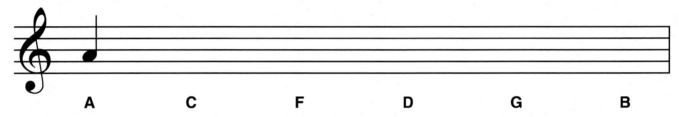

A   C   F   D   G   B

Draw a **quarter note** F
which is higher than the
note printed on the **staff**.

Draw a **half note** A
which is lower than the
note printed on the **staff**.

Draw a **whole note** C
which is higher than the
note printed on the **staff**.

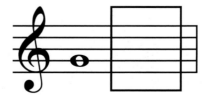

LESSON 2 *Note Names in the Bass Clef*

Now let's name the lines and spaces in the **bass clef**.

Do you remember that the **bass clef** is also known as the **F clef**? Here's why: the two dots, above and below the 4th line, tell us that the tell us that the 4th line is an F.

Here is F in the **bass clef**:

← 4th line = F

If we know where to find F in the **bass clef**, we can find every other note in the **staff**. Remember: after G, we start the alphabet over again with A. Going up:

F   G   A   B

Notice that the space above the top line has a letter name.

Going down, we'll have to go backwards in the alphabet from F, like this:

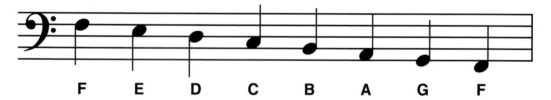

F   E   D   C   B   A   G   F

Notice that the space below the bottom line has a letter name.

Here are all the letter names of the lines and spaces in the **bass clef**.

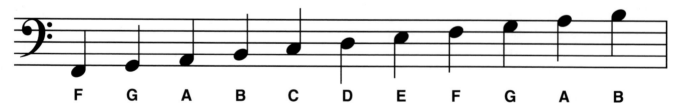

F   G   A   B   C   D   E   F   G   A   B

The spaces, from bottom to top, are A-C-E-G. Some people remember these because it is the first letter from each word in the sentence, "*All cows eat grass.*"

The lines, from bottom to top, are G-B-D-F-A. Some people remember these because it is the first letter from each word in the sentence, "*Good boys do fine always.*"

LESSON 2 REVIEW   *Note Names in the Bass Clef*

Place the correct letter name under each **note** in the **bass clef**.

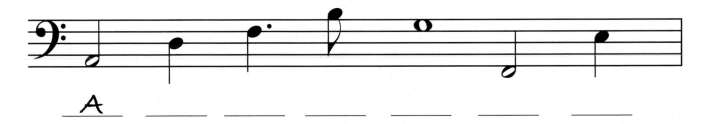

A _____ _____ _____ _____ _____ _____ _____

Draw **quarter notes** in the **bass clef** for each of the following letter names. Don't forget to draw the **stem** correctly. (In some cases there may be more than one correct answer.)

B   **D**   **F**   **A**   **C**   **E**

Draw a **quarter note** F
which is higher than the
note printed on the **staff**.

Draw a **half note** A
which is lower than the
note printed on the **staff.**

Draw a **whole note** E
which is higher than the
note printed on the **staff**.

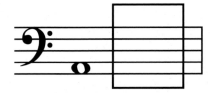

LESSON 3 *Ledger Lines*

Notes (and musical sounds) don't end above and below a **staff**.
The **notes** can continue going higher, like this:

Or lower, like this:

The short lines used for these **notes** are called **ledger lines** (pronounced LEH-jur lines). **Notes** are placed on, above, or below the **ledger lines**. **Ledger lines** are really just a continuation of the **staff**, but the lines are shorter. They don't run all the way across the page like **staff** lines.

The letter names of the **notes** continue up and down on the **ledger lines**. Here are the **note** names for **ledger lines** in the **treble clef**.

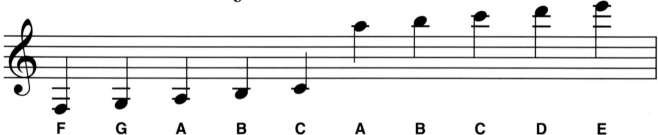

Here are the **note** names for **ledger lines** in the **bass clef**.

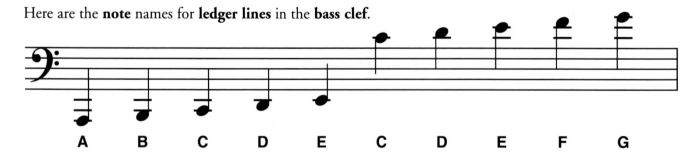

We've only shown three **ledger lines** in these examples, but they can continue for more than three. Sometimes you may see four or even five **ledger lines**.

Note: **ledger lines** can also be spelled **leger lines**.

LESSON 3
REVIEW   *Ledger Lines*

What are the letter names of these **notes** in the **treble clef**? Place the answer on the line below the **staff**.

———   ———   ———   ———

What are the letter names of these **notes** in the **bass clef**? Place the answer on the line belopw the **staff**.

———   ———   ———   ———

Use **ledger lines** to draw the correct **notes** in the box.

This is a **half note** A. To its right, draw another **half note** A above the **staff**.

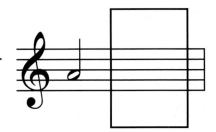

Now draw a **half note** A below the **staff**.

Here is a **whole note** D. To its right, draw another **whole note** D below the **staff**.

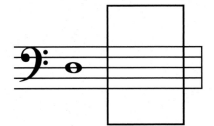

Now draw a **whole note** D above the **staff**.

Circle the correct **note** for the questions below.

Which **note** is a B?

Which **note** is a C?

LESSON 4   *Grand Staff*

Sometimes the **treble clef** and the **bass clef** are combined, like this:

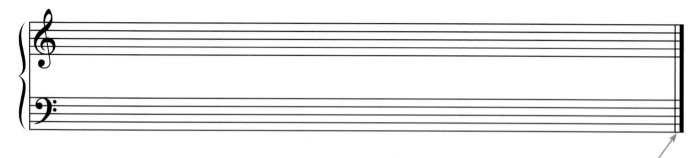

Piano players read notes on the combined **treble** and **bass clefs** like this, which is sometimes called a **grand staff**.

This is a double barline. It appears at the end of a piece of music.

Here's what music looks like on the the **grand staff**.

Minuet

Jean Phillipe Rameau
(1683–1764)

This piece of music for piano was written by a French composer named Jean Phillipe Rameau. The composer of a piece of music is always listed at the top right, above the first **staff**.

LESSON 4 *Grand Staff*

If you have a piano, or your music room has a piano, you can see how the **notes** on the piano match up with the **note** names on the **grand staff.**

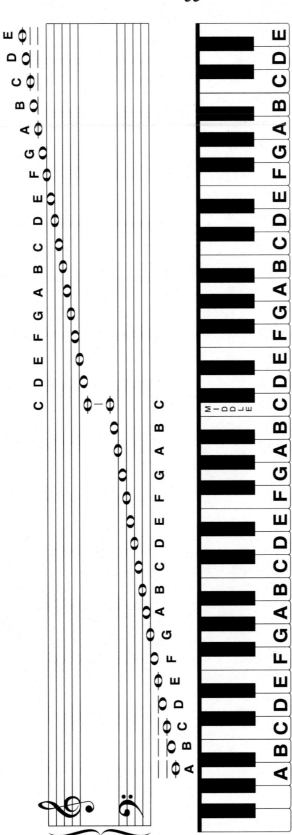

Notice that the first **ledger line** below the **treble clef** is a C, and that the first **ledger line** above the **bass clef** is also a C. On a **grand staff**, it's the same **note**, and is known as "middle C."

LESSON 5 *Sharp and Flat*

Sometimes you will see a musical symbol before a **note** on the **staff**, like this:

Or like this:

Sharp

This musical symbol is called a **sharp**. A **sharp** means that the **note** should be played or sung just a little bit higher. (Music readers call that "little bit" a half step.)

Flat

This musical symbol is called a **flat**. A **flat** means that the **note** should be played or sung just a little bit lower. (Music readers call that "little bit" a half step.)

Examples:

This **note** is a C.

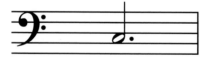

This **note** is a C♯ (C-sharp.) It is sung or played a little bit higher —a half step higher—than a C.

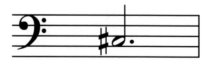

This **note** is an E.

This **note** is an E♭ (E-flat.) It is sung or played a little bit lower —a half step lower—than an E.

LESSON 5 *Sharp and Flat*

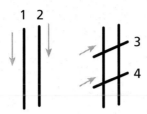

Here's how to draw a **sharp**.

Here's how to draw a **flat**.

When a **sharp** is placed on a **staff** line, it looks like this:

When a **flat** is placed on a **staff** line, it looks like this:

When a **sharp** is placed in a **staff** space, it looks like this:

When a **flat** is placed in a **staff** space, it looks like this:

Practice drawing **sharps** by drawing a **sharp** on the line or in the space shown below:

On the 2nd line   On the 5th line   In the 3rd space   On the 2nd line   In the 3rd space

Practice drawing **flats** by drawing a **flat** on the line or in the space shown below:

In the 2nd space   On the 3rd line   In the 4th space   On the 4th line   On the 1st line

LESSON 5
REVIEW
Sharp and Flat

Name the following **notes** in the **treble clef**.

_____ _____ _____ _____ _____

Name the following **notes** in the **bass clef**.

_____ _____ _____ _____

Circle the **note** which is higher.    Circle the **note** which is lower.

Using **quarter notes**, write the following **notes** in the **treble clef**.
(There will be more than one correct answer.)

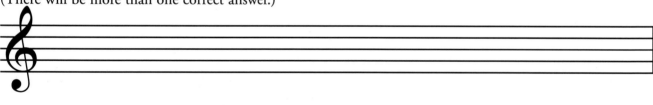

B♭   **G♯**   **D♭**   **F♯**   **C♯**

Using **half notes**, write the following **notes** in the **bass clef**.
(There will be more than one correct answer.)

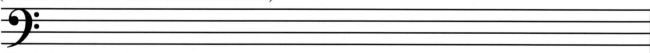

A♯   **D♯**   **G♭**   **E♭**   **C♯**

LESSON 6 *Key Signatures*

Suppose a composer wrote a song and wanted it to sound like this:

There are a lot of **flats** in this song!

There's an easier way to write this song. The composer can put all the **flats** at the beginning of every **staff**. This way, music readers know to sing or play all the **flats** which are shown on every **staff**. So it looks like this:

Here's another example:

Instead of putting a **sharp** in front of every F, the composer has placed one **sharp**, on the fourth line, at the beginning of every **staff**. **Sharps** or **flats** at the beginning of a **staff** are called a **key signature**.

Here are some common **key signatures** using **flats**:

LESSON 6 *Key Signatures*

Here are some common **key signatures** using **sharps**.

MUSICAL RULE — A **key signature** will have all **flats** or all **sharps**.
It will never have both **sharps** *and* **flats**.

MUSICAL RULE — If an F♯ is in a **key signature**, then all F's in the **staff** will be **sharp.**
The same is true of any other **notes** for which there is a **sharp** or **flat** in the **key signature**.

Examples:

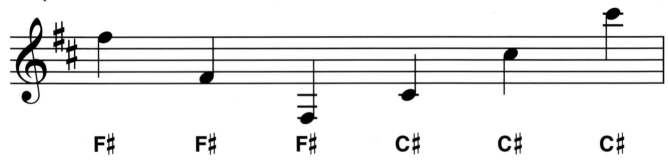

Every F and every C is **sharp**.

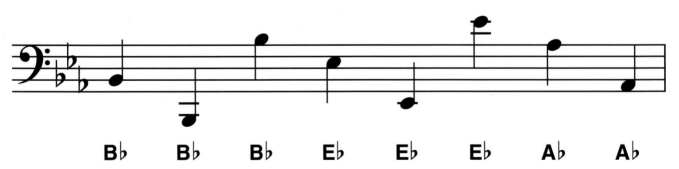

Every B, every E, and every A is **flat**.

LESSON 6
REVIEW *Key Signatures*

Look at the musical examples on the left. These examples have **sharps** or **flats** but no **key signature**. In the **staff** on the right, draw the same **notes**, without **sharps** or **flats**, and add the correct **key signature**.

 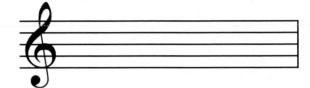

 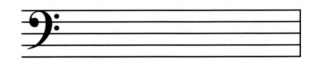

Draw the **key signature** with three **flats**. We've drawn the first **flat** for you.

Draw the **key signature** with three **sharps**. We've drawn the first **sharp** for you.

Below are three pairs of **key signatures**. In each pair, one is drawn correctly and one is drawn incorrectly. Circle the correct **key signature** in each pair.

1.    OR

2. 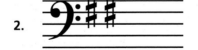   OR

3.    OR

LESSON 7 *Naming Key Signatures*

The **flats** or **sharps** in a **key signature** follow a pattern. Here's the pattern for **sharp key signatures**:

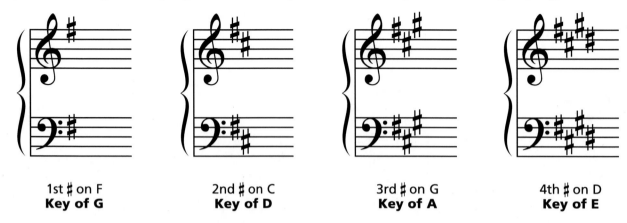

| 1st ♯ on F | 2nd ♯ on C | 3rd ♯ on G | 4th ♯ on D |
| **Key of G** | **Key of D** | **Key of A** | **Key of E** |

Here's the pattern for **flat key signatures**:

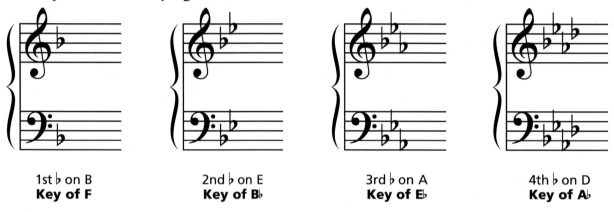

| 1st ♭ on B | 2nd ♭ on E | 3rd ♭ on A | 4th ♭ on D |
| **Key of F** | **Key of B♭** | **Key of E♭** | **Key of A♭** |

There can be as many as seven **flats** or **sharps** in a **key signature**, but you'll rarely see more than four. For this book, we'll use no more than four.

Every **key signature** is named after a **note** (and every **note** has a **key signature**). A piece of music is said to be in the "key of G" or the "key of B♭" and so forth. We've labeled the **key signature** names for the eight keys shown above. Here's how to identify **key signatures**.

For **sharp key signatures**, find the last **sharp** in the **key signature**. Then count up to the next line or space. That **note** is the name of the **key signature**.

For **flat key signatures**, find the last **flat** in the **key signature**. Think of this as "four," then count down the lines and spaces of the **staff** to "one." The note on "one" is the name for the **key signature**.

What if a piece of music has no **key signature**... no **sharps** or **flats** after the **clef sign**? Music with no **key signature** is the key of C.

LESSON 7
REVIEW *Naming Key Signatures*

Identify the following **key signatures**.
Write the correct name of each **key signature** on the line provided.

1.  _____

4.  _____

2.  _____

5.  _____

3.  _____

6. 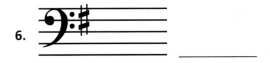 _____

In the box, write the correct **sharps** for the following **sharp key signatures**.

1.

Key of G

2.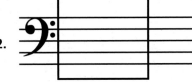

Key of A

In the box, write the correct **flats** for the following **flat key signatures**.

1.

Key of B♭

2.

Key of F

LESSON 8   *Natural Sign and Accidentals*

Sometimes, even with a **key signature**, **flats** and **sharps** have to be added in a piece of music. Look at this piece of music which has **flats** in the **key signature** and **sharps** in front of several **notes**.

Suppose a composer wrote a song with a **key signature** of two **sharps** but wanted this **note** ———— to be an F instead of an F♯.

The composer would place a different musical symbol, called a **natural**, in front of the F, like this:

A **natural** tells a music reader not to sing or play the **flat** or **sharp** shown in the **key signature**. In this example, the note in the box is called an F♮ (F-natural.) The **natural** sign "erases" the F♯ in the **key signature**...*but only for that one **measure***.

Here's how to draw a **natural**.

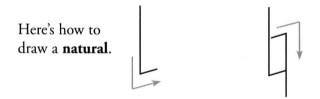

When **sharps**, **flats**, and **natural** signs are placed throughout a piece of music they are called **accidentals**. **Accidentals** last for one **measure**. In other words, **accidentals** are "erased" by a **barline**.

Key Signature   **Accidentals**   **Barline** cancels the **accidentals** in previous **measure**

LESSON 8
REVIEW
Natural Sign and Accidentals

What **note** is in the box? Circle the correct answer.

1.   F   or   F♯

2.   B♭   or   B

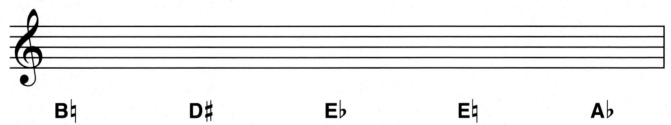

3.   G   or   G♯

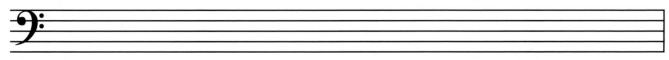

4.   A♮   or   A♭

Using **half notes**, draw the following **notes** in the **treble clef**. There will be more than one correct answer.

B♮   **D♯**   **E♭**   **E♮**   **A♭**

Using **quarter notes**, draw the following **notes** in the **bass clef**. There will be more than one correct answer.

G♯   **C♯**   **F♮**   **C♮**   **A♭**

UNIT 4
More Musical Symbols and Terms

LESSON 1 *How Loud? How Soft?*

We have learned that **notes** tell music readers how high or low to sing or play a musical sound, and how long or short to sing or play a musical sound. There is one more thing we need to know when we sing or play music: how loud or soft to sing or play it. Musical symbols known as **dynamics** tell us how loud or soft to perform music.

The **dynamic symbol** for loud is called **forte** (FOR-tay), and looks like the letter f.

f

The **dynamic symbol** for soft is called **piano** (Pe-AH-no, the same as the musical instrument) and looks like the letter p.

p

The **dynamic symbol** for very loud is two **forte** symbols. This is called **fortissimo** (for-TEE-see-mo).

ff

The **dynamic symbol** for very soft is two **piano** symbols. This is called **pianissimo** (pe-ah-NEE-see-mo).

pp

There are **dynamic symbols** for medium loud and medium soft, too. For medium loud, an "m" is placed in front of the **forte** symbol. The "m" stands for mezzo (MET-tzo), an Italian word meaning medium or moderately. So the symbol is called **mezzo forte** (MET-tzo FOR-tay).

mf

The symbol for medium soft is **mezzo piano** (MET-tzo pe-AH-no).

mp

The words for the **dynamic symbols** are all Italian. Now you know five Italian words: **forte** (loud), **piano** (soft), **fortissimo** (very loud), **pianissimo** (very soft), and **mezzo** (medium).

Dynamics are usually placed **below** a **staff**, like this. The music is performed at one **dynamic** level until a different **dynamic** is shown.

Here's a chart of **dynamics**, from softest to loudest:

pp   *p*   *mp*   *mf*   *f*   *ff*

softest - → loudest

LESSON 1
REVIEW
How Loud? How Soft?

Which **dynamic level** is louder? Circle the correct answer.

1. *p*   or   *mp*   3. *f*   or   *p*

2. *ff*   or   *pp*   4. *mf*   or   *mp*

Which **dynamic level** is softer? Circle the correct answer.

1. *p*   or   *f*   3. *ff*   or   *f*

2. *mp*   or   *mf*   4. *f*   or   *mp*

What does each **dynamic level** mean? Write the correct letter from the second column in the blank space.

1. _____ *p*   A.   Loud

2. _____ *mf*   B.   Very soft

3. _____ *ff*   C.   Medium loud

4. _____ *mp*   D.   Medium soft

5. _____ *f*   E.   Very loud

6. _____ *pp*   F.   Soft

Match the Italian term with each **dynamic level**.

1. _____ *p*   A.   *pianissimo*

2. _____ *mf*   B.   *piano*

3. _____ *ff*   C.   *mezzo piano*

4. _____ *mp*   D.   *mezzo forte*

5. _____ *f*   E.   *forte*

6. _____ *pp*   F.   *fortissimo*

LESSON 2   *More About Loud and Soft*

Sometimes music gradually changes from soft to loud, or from loud to soft.
The most common **dynamic** symbols to show a change in volume look like this:

A **crescendo** (creh-SHEN-doh) sign
means to gradually get louder.

A **decrescendo** (deh-creh-SHEN-doh)
sign means to gradually get softer.
Sometimes this sign is called a
diminuendo (dih-min-you-EHN-doh).

Sometimes **crescendo** and **decrescendo** signs are called **wedges** or **hairpins**.
But music readers usually call them **crescendo** and **decrescendo** signs.

Crescendo and **decrescendo** signs are usually placed below the **staff**, like this:

Sometimes you might see the words *crescendo, decrescendo,* or *diminuendo*
(or their abbreviations shown below) instead of the symbols.

to gradually
get louder

= *crescendo* = *cresc.*

to gradually
get softer

= *decrescendo* = *decresc.*
or *diminuendo*   or *dim.*

LESSON 2 *More About Loud and Soft*
REVIEW

Write the correct answer in the blank space.

1. *Decrescendo* means the same as _____

    A. *Diminuendo*

    B. *Crescendo*

2. ⟨⟩ means _____

    A. to gradually get louder

    B. to gradually get softer

In the examples below, are the **dynamics** correct or incorrect?
Circle the correct answer.

1.   Correct   or   Incorrect

2.   Correct   or   Incorrect

3.   Correct   or   Incorrect

How loud or soft is the music at Ⓐ Ⓑ Ⓒ and Ⓓ? Circle the correct answer.

Ⓐ   Soft   or   Loud

Ⓑ   Medium loud or   Medium soft

Ⓒ   Very soft   or   Medium soft

Ⓓ   Very loud   or   Very soft

LESSON 3 — *How Fast? How Slow?*

You have learned that musical **notes** can be high or low, long or short, and loud or soft.
You also need to know how fast or how slow the music should be played or sung.
This is called the **tempo** of the music.

Often, a word or two at the beginning of a piece of music will tell you how fast it
should be played. But sometimes, **tempo** markings, like **dynamic** markings, are
shown with Italian words. Here are some common **tempo** markings:

Largo   (LAHR-go)   = very slow

Adagio   (Ah-DAH-jhee-oh) = slow

Andante   (Ahn-DAHN-tay)   = a moderate speed, often called a walking **tempo**

Moderato   (Mohd-air-AH-to) = moderately, but faster than **andante**

Allegro   (Ah-LEG-roh)   = fast

Vivace   (Vee-VAH-chay)   = very fast

Presto   (PRESS-toh)   = very fast, faster than **vivace**

There are musical terms (and abbreviations) for changes in **tempo**, too:

Ritardando (ree-tahr-DAHN-doh) or **rit.**   = gradually slower

Rallentando (rahl-ehn-TAHN-doh) or **rall.**   = gradually slower

Accelerando (ack-shell-air-AHN-doh) or **accel.** = gradually faster

a tempo (ah TEHM-po)   = return to previous tempo

Tempo markings are usually placed above the **staff**.
Changes in **tempo** are usually placed below the **staff**.

Here's a chart of **tempos** from slowest to fastest:

Largo	Adagio	Andante	Moderato	Allegro	Vivace	Presto

slowest- →fastest

LESSON 3
REVIEW
How Fast? How Slow?

Which **tempo marking** is faster? Circle the correct answer.

1. *Largo*   or   *Presto*   **2.** *Vivace*   or   *Adagio*

Which **tempo marking** is slower? Circle the correct answer.

1. *Presto*   or   *Andante*   **2.** *Moderato*   or   *Vivace*

What does each **tempo marking** mean?
Write the correct letter from the second column in the blank space.

1. _____	*Allegro*	A.	Fast
2. _____	*Vivace*	B.	Very slow
3. _____	*Andante*	C.	Walking tempo
4. _____	*Largo*	D.	A moderate speed
5. _____	*Moderato*	E.	Very fast
6. _____	*Adagio*	F.	Slow

What does each of these **tempo changes** mean?
Write the correct letter from the second column in the blank space.

1. _____	*ritardando*	A.	gradually slower
2. _____	*accelerando*	B.	gradually faster
3. _____	*a tempo*	C.	return to previous tempo

LESSON 4 *Staccato and Fermata*

Sometimes you will see other musical symbols placed above or below a **notehead**. These markings are called **articulations**. **Articulations** tell music readers how a **note** should be played or sung. In this lesson and in the next lesson you will learn several **articulations**.

This is a **staccato** (stah-KAH-toh) dot. A **note** with a **staccato** dot should be played or sung very short. It should be separated from the **note** after it.

Here's an example of a piece of music using short, **staccato notes**.

MUSICAL RULE - **Staccato** dots are always placed near the **notehead**. If the stem is down, the **staccato** dot is above the **notehead**. If the **stem** is up, the **staccato** dot is below the **notehead**.

Here's a musical symbol which is the opposite of a **staccato** dot.

This is a **fermata** (fehr-MAH-tah). A **note** with a **fermata** above it is held much longer than the **note** would normally be held. In fact, the **beat** or pulse of the music stops, and doesn't start again until the performer stops holding the **note** with the **fermata**.

The **quarter note** with the **fermata** is held much longer than a normal **quarter note**. The **half note** with the **fermata** is held much longer than a normal **half note**.

MUSICAL RULE - A **fermata** is always placed above the **note** and above the **staff**.

LESSON 4
REVIEW
Staccato and Fermata

Which **note** is shorter? Circle the correct answer.

Which **note** is longer? Circle the correct answer.

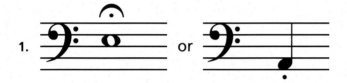 

Place a **staccato** dot on every G♯ in this example.
Be sure to position it correctly, either above or below the **notehead**.

Place a **fermata** over every **half note** in this example.

LESSON 5   *Accent, Tenuto, and Marcato*

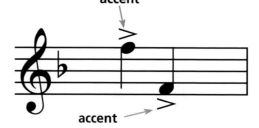

This mark (>) is called an **accent** (AK-sent).
An **accent** means the **note** should be played
or sung loudly.

The **notes** with **accents** should be played or sung louder than the others.

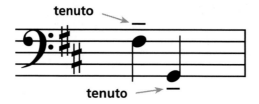

This mark (–) is called a
tenuto (teh-NOO-toh) mark.
It has two meanings.

1) A **tenuto** mark can mean to play a **note** slightly
   louder, but not quite as loudly as an **accent**.

2) It can also tell the music reader to play
   or sing a **note** for its full value.

MUSICAL RULE — **Accents** and **tenuto** marks are always placed near the
notehead. If the **stem** is down, the **accent** or **tenuto** mark is above the **notehead**.
If the **stem** is up, the **accent** or **tenuto** mark is below the **notehead**.

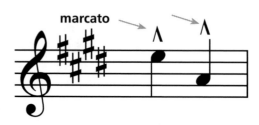

This mark (∧) is called **marcato** (mar-KAH-toh).
It means to play a note *very* loudly...even
louder than an > **accent**.

MUSICAL RULE — **Marcato** marks are always placed above the **note**.
It doesn't matter if the **stem** goes up or down, the **marcato** mark is always above.

Look at some of the **articulations** in this piece of music. Notice that **articulations** can be combined.

LESSON 5
REVIEW *Accent, Tenuto, and Marcato*

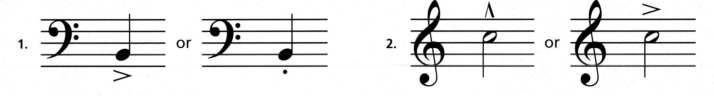

Which **note** is louder? Circle the correct answer.

1.   [bass clef note with > accent] or [bass clef note with staccato dot]   2.   [treble clef note with ∧ marcato] or [treble clef note with > accent]

What does each mark mean?
Write the correct letter from the second column in the blank space.

1. _____   ∧   A. Loud

2. _____   >   B. Louder

3. _____   —   C. Loudest

Place an **>** **accent** on every B♭ in this example.
Be sure to position it correctly, either above or below the **notehead**.

Place a **marcato** mark over every **eighth note** in this example.

LESSON 6 *Repeats, First and Second Endings*

Sometimes, the composer of a piece of music will want to repeat a section of the music. Instead of writing out all the **measures** again, the composer uses musical symbols called **repeat signs** to tell a music reader to repeat a section of the music. **Repeat signs** look like this:

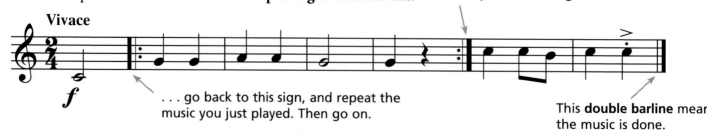

When you see this sign...

. . . go back to this sign, and repeat the music you just played. Then go on.

This **double barline** means the music is done.

If no beginning **repeat sign** is shown (‖:), go back to the beginning of the piece.

You will also see these symbols, known as a **first ending** and a **second ending**.

Play this **measure** the first time only.

On the repeat, skip from here...   ...to here.

Here is an example of music using **repeat signs**, a **first ending**, and a **second ending**.

LESSON 7   *Vocal Music*

When a singer reads music, he or she also has to read the words which must be sung.

The words of a piece of music are placed below the **notes**, like this:

Notice that when words are below the **staff**, the **dynamic marking** is placed *above* the **staff**.

If a piano plays along with the singer, the **staff** with the words
is above the **grand staff** for the piano, like this:

This is a **slur**. It means to sing one word over two or more notes.

LESSON 8 · *Putting It All Together*

L'il 'Liza Jane

American Folk Song
Arranged by **JAY ALTHOUSE**

The Symbols of Music

Staff

Treble Clef
(G Clef)

Bass Clef
(F Clef)

Whole Note

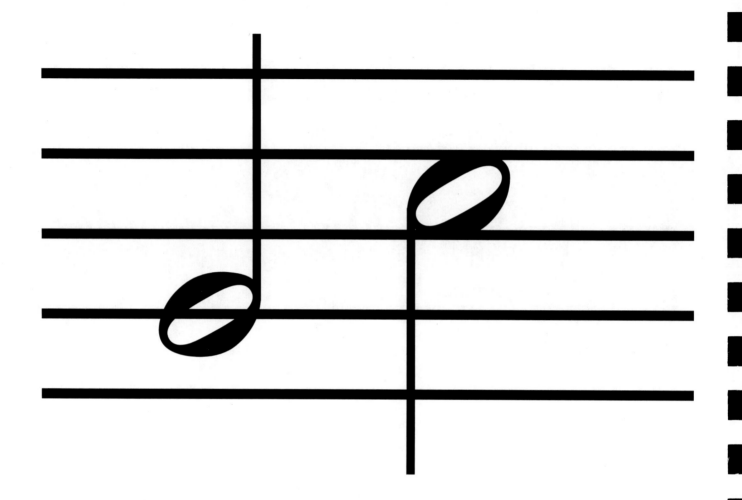

Half Notes

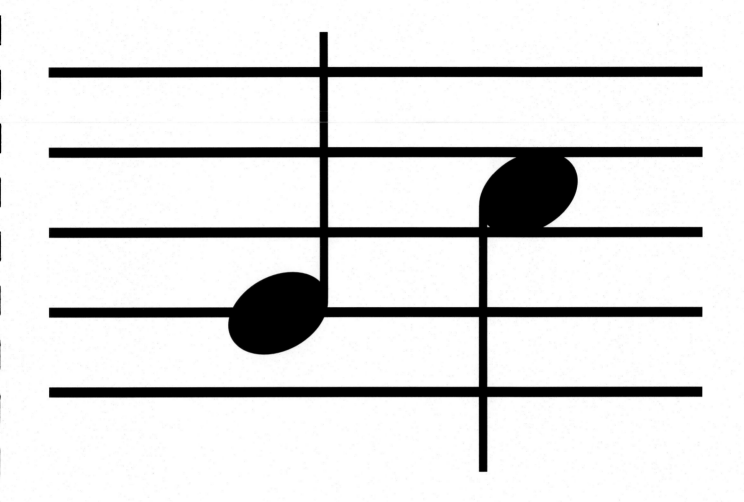

Quarter Notes

Eighth Notes

Whole Rest

Half Rest

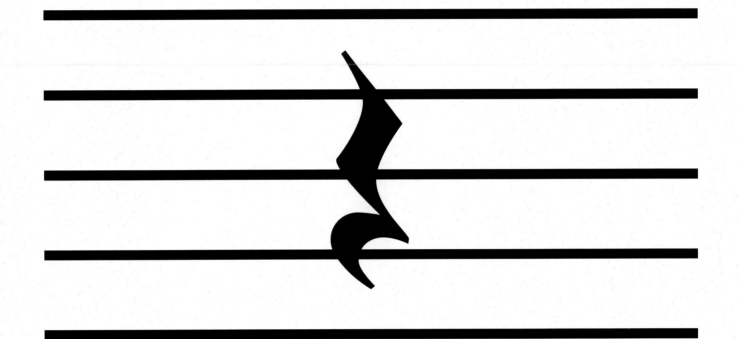

Quarter Rest

Eighth Rest

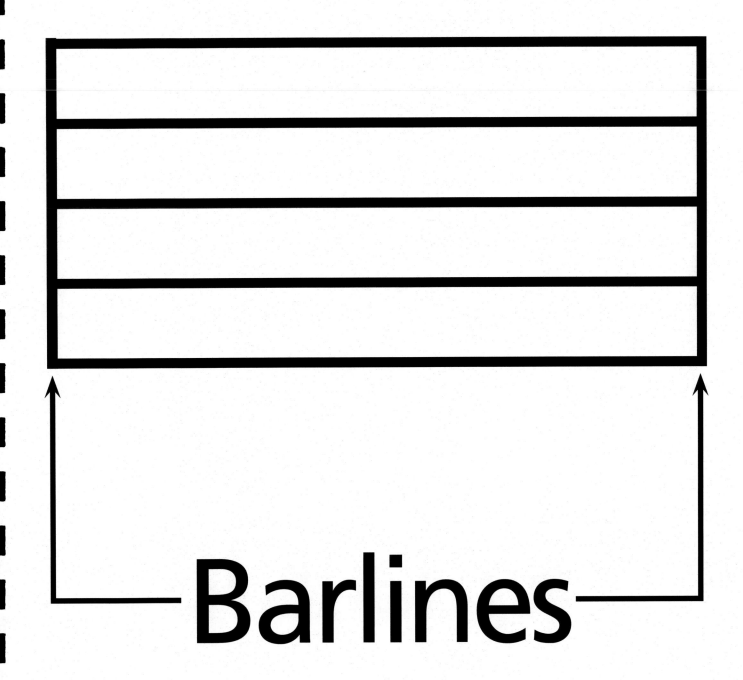

Barlines

Measure

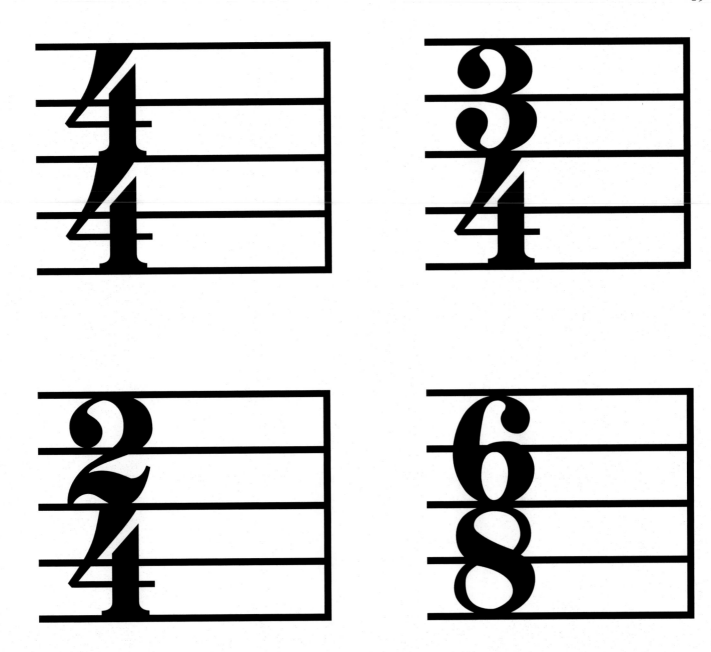

Time Signatures

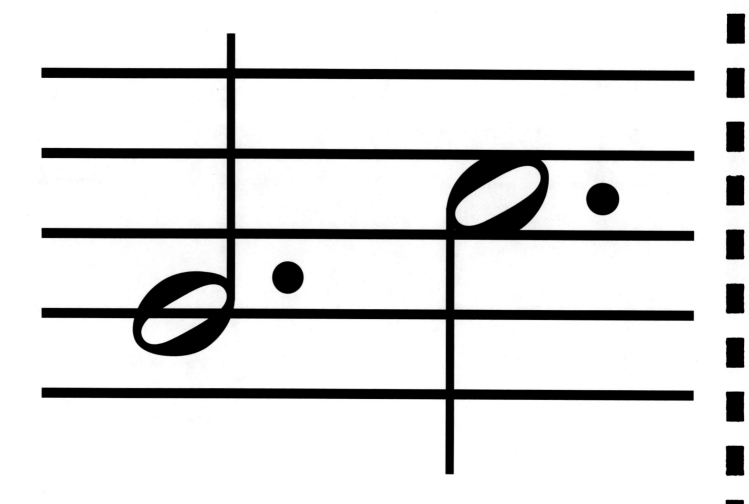

Dotted
Half Notes

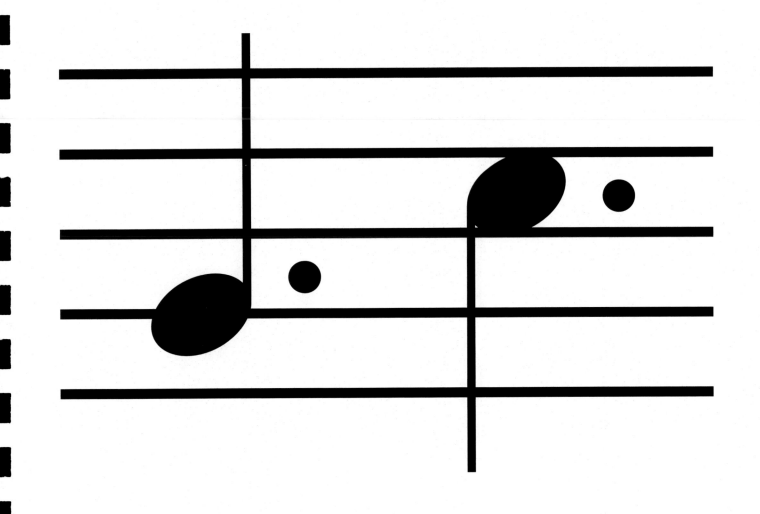

Dotted
Quarter Notes

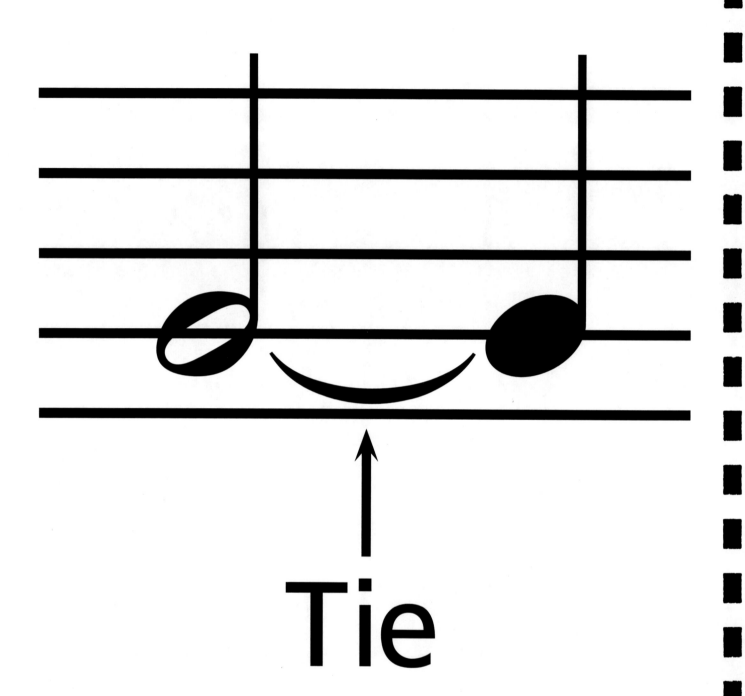

Tie

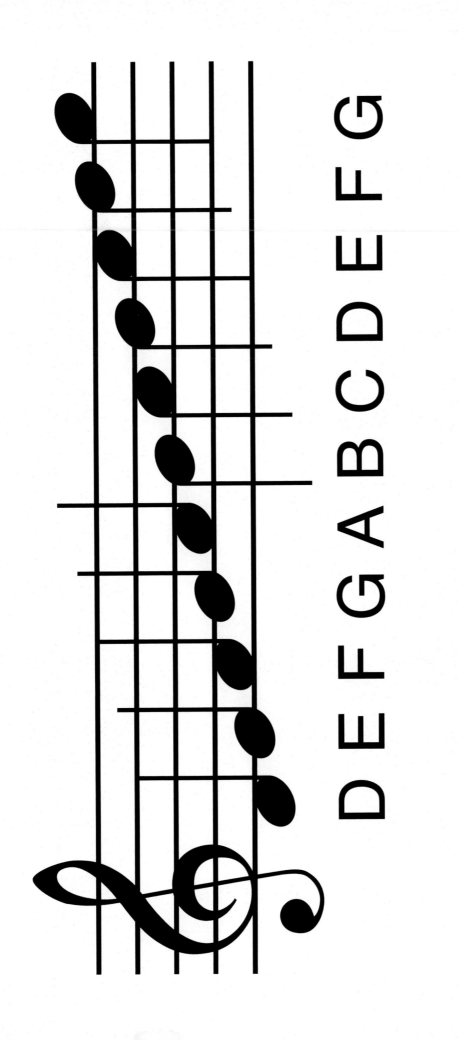

Note Names in Treble Clef

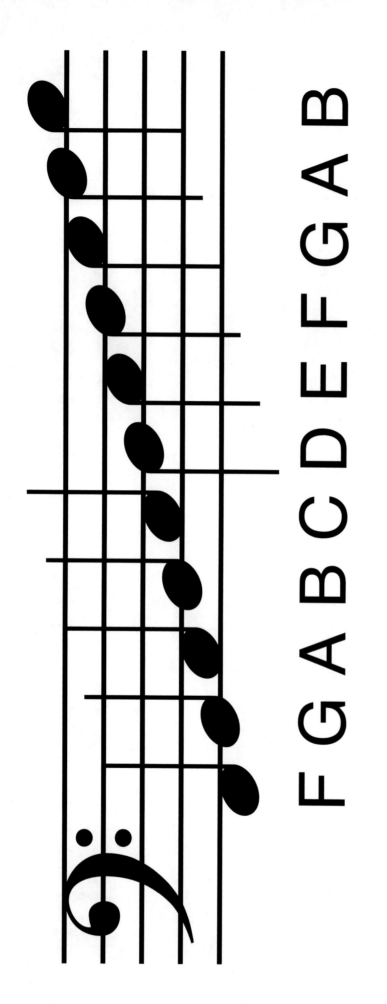

Note Names in Bass Clef

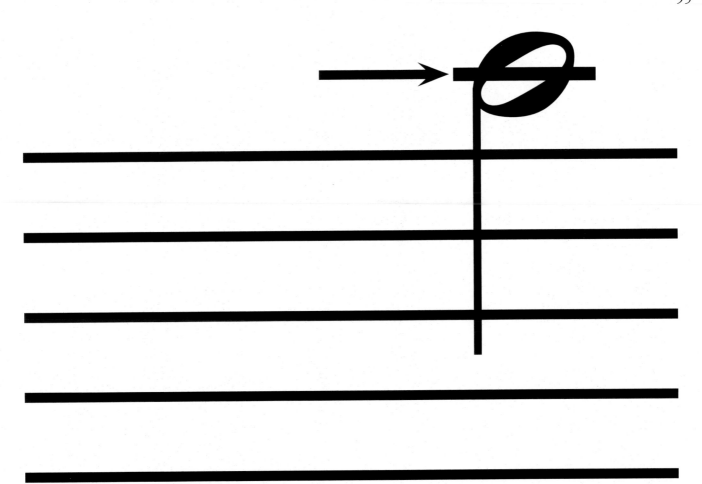

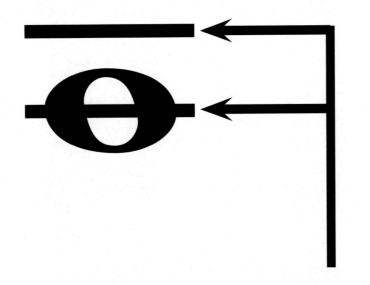

Ledger Lines

Grand Staff

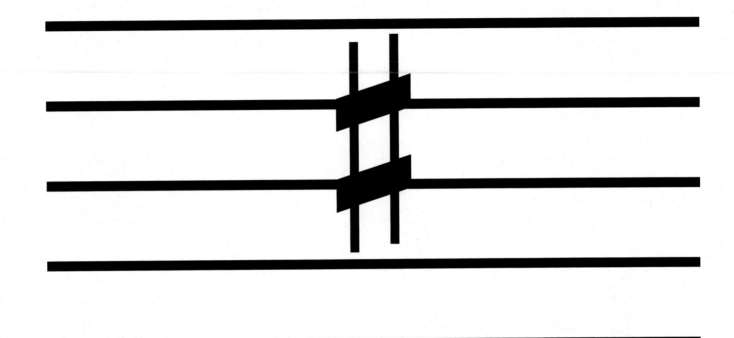

Sharp

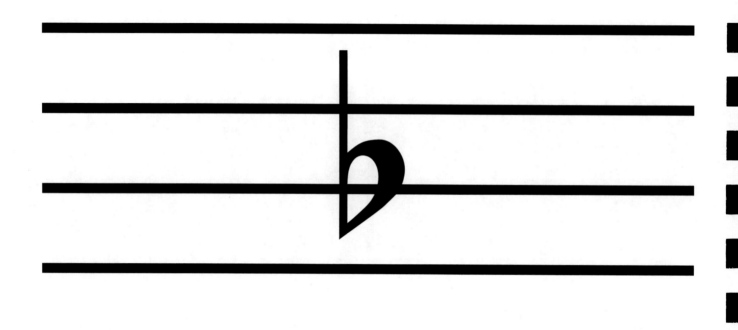

Flat

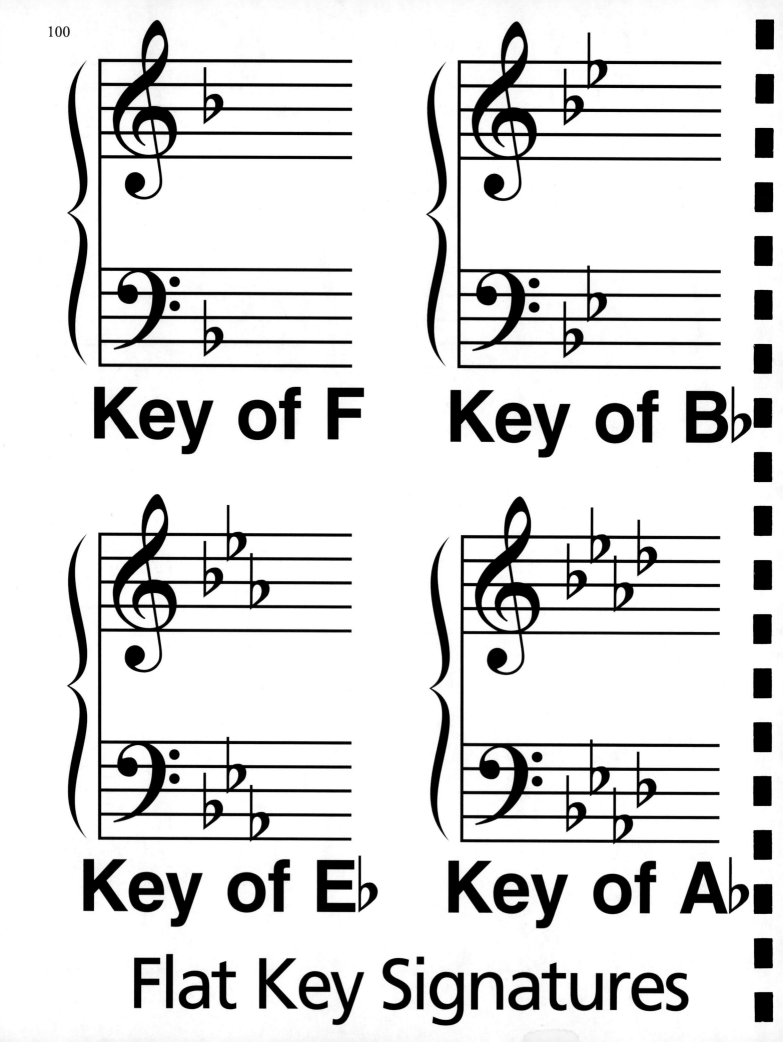

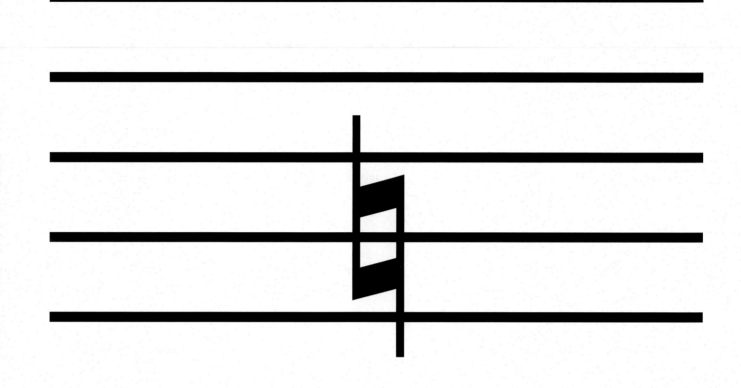

Natural

Loudest

ff	*fortissimo*
f	*forte*
mf	*mezzo forte*
mp	*mezzo piano*
p	*piano*
pp	*pianissimo*

Softest

Dynamics

To gradually get louder

crescendo
cresc.

To gradually get softer

decrescendo
decresc.

or *diminuendo*
dim.

More Dynamics

Fastest

Presto

Vivace

Allegro

Moderato

Andante

Adagio

Largo

Slowest

Tempos

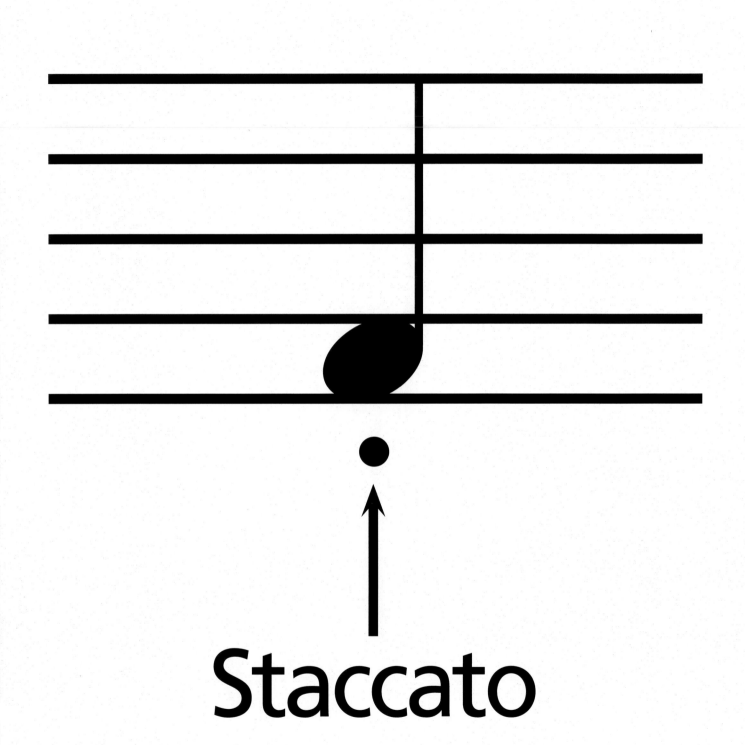

Staccato

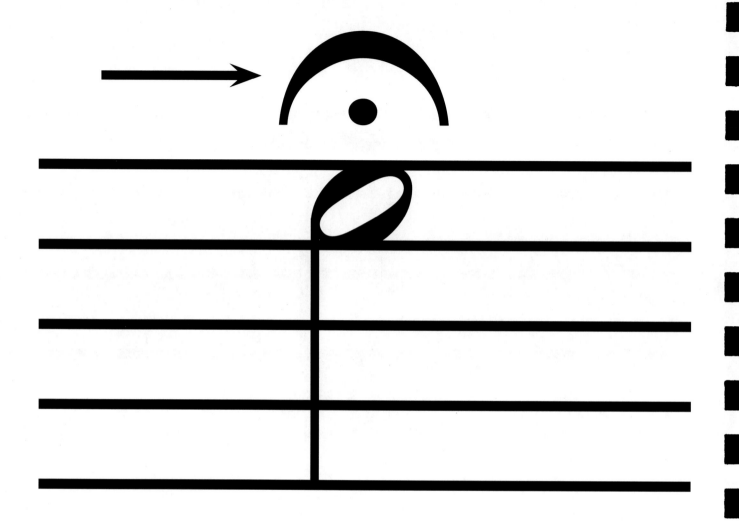

Fermata

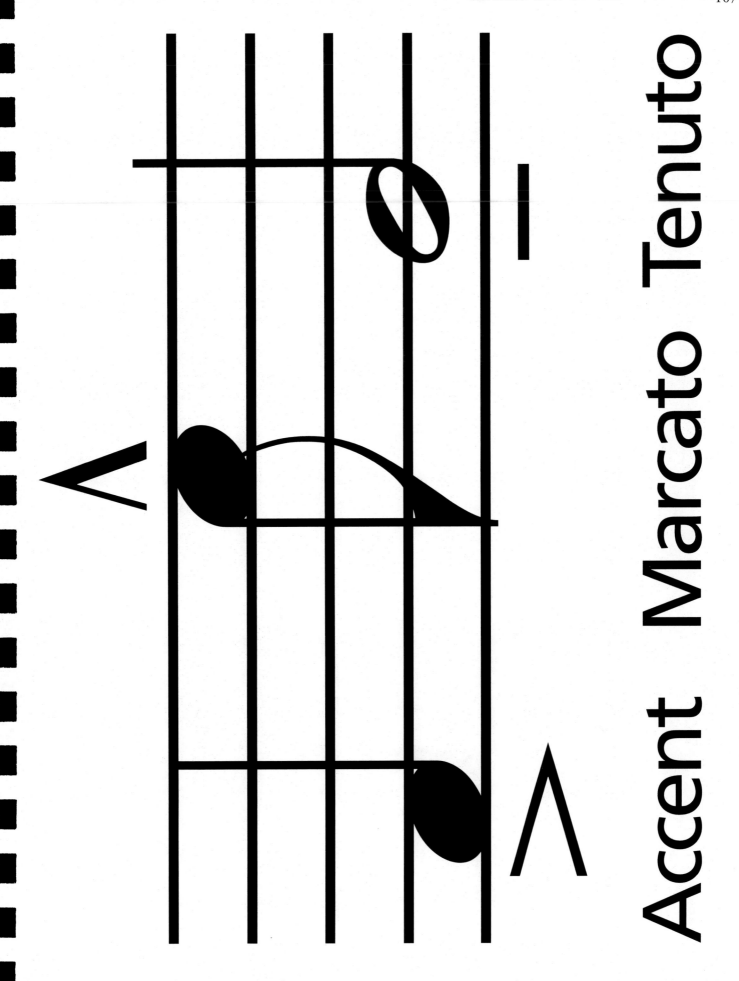

Accent Marcato Tenuto

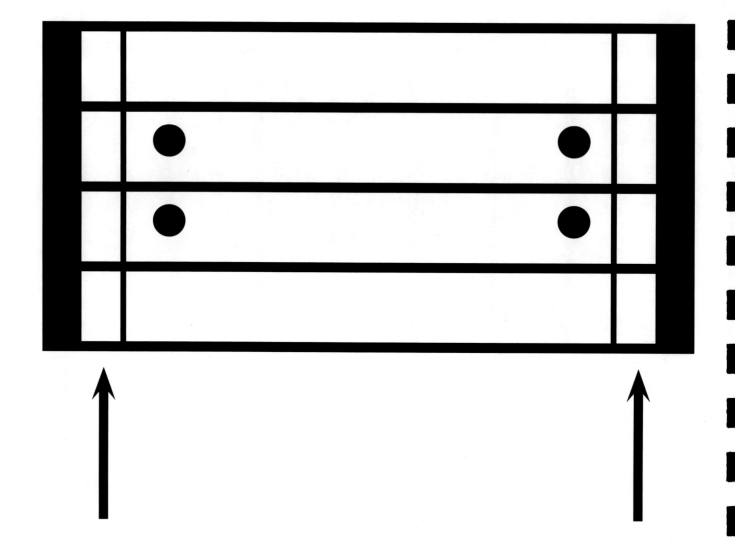

Repeat Signs

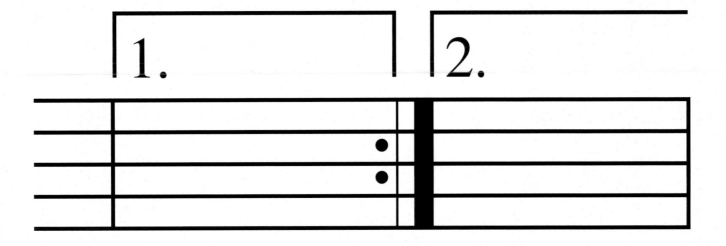

First Ending
Second Ending

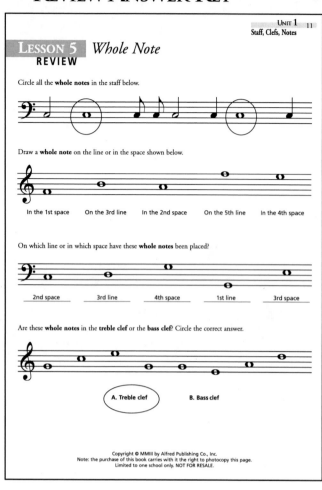

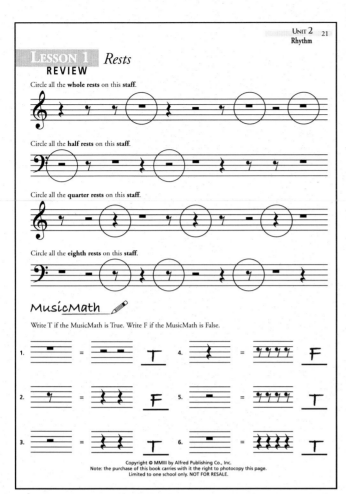

LESSON 1 — Rests
REVIEW

Circle all the **whole rests** on this staff.

Circle all the **half rests** on this staff.

Circle all the **quarter rests** on this staff.

Circle all the **eighth rests** on this staff.

MusicMath

Write T if the MusicMath is True. Write F if the MusicMath is False.

1. = **T**
2. = **F**
3. = **T**
4. = **F**
5. = **T**
6. = **T**

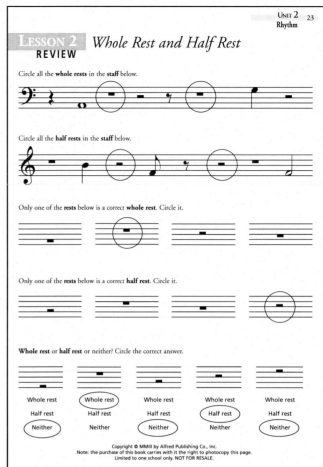

LESSON 2 — Whole Rest and Half Rest
REVIEW

Circle all the **whole rests** in the staff below.

Circle all the **half rests** in the staff below.

Only one of the **rests** below is a correct **whole rest**. Circle it.

Only one of the **rests** below is a correct **half rest**. Circle it.

Whole rest or **half rest** or neither? Circle the correct answer.

Whole rest	(Whole rest)	Whole rest	Whole rest	Whole rest
Half rest	Half rest	Half rest	(Half rest)	Half rest
(Neither)	Neither	(Neither)	Neither	(Neither)

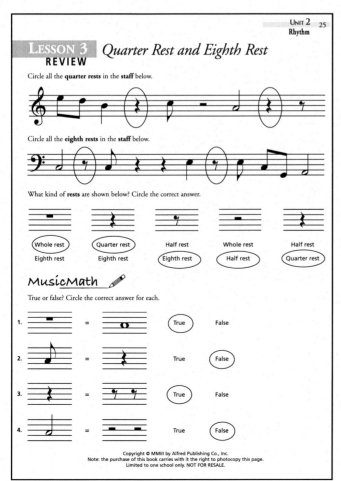

LESSON 3 — Quarter Rest and Eighth Rest
REVIEW

Circle all the **quarter rests** in the **staff** below.

Circle all the **eighth rests** in the **staff** below.

What kind of **rests** are shown below? Circle the correct answer.

| Whole rest | Quarter rest | Half rest | Whole rest | Half rest |
| (Eighth rest) | Eighth rest | (Eighth rest) | (Half rest) | (Quarter rest) |

MusicMath

True or false? Circle the correct answer for each.

1. = (True)   False
2. = True   (False)
3. = (True)   False
4. = True   (False)

LESSON 4 — Barlines and Measures
REVIEW

Circle the second **note** in the second **measure** and the third **note** in the fourth **measure**.

Rests can be written in place of **notes** in a **measure**, like this.
Circle every **half note** and every **half rest** in this example.

Put three **quarter notes** and one one **quarter rest** in each **measure**, using the instructions below the staff. Place the **quarter notes** anywhere on the **staff**, some on lines and some in **spaces**.

note note note rest   note rest note note   rest note note note

Using **barlines**, divide the **staff** below into four **measures**.
Then place one **half note** and one **half rest** in each **measure**.

MusicMath

The first **measure** has a **whole note**. The second **measure** has two **half notes**. Place four **notes** in the third **measure** that equal the value of the **notes** in the first two **measures**.

What kind of **note** did you place in the third **measure**?   **Quarter note**

LESSON 5 *Beats*
REVIEW

If a **quarter note** gets one **beat**, how many **beats** are there in this **measure**?

If a **half note** gets one **beat**, how many **beats** are in this **measure**?

If an **eighth note** gets one **beat**, how many **beats** are in this **measure**?

In the **staff** below, a **quarter note** gets one **beat**. Place **barlines** after every three **beats**.

In the **staff** below, a **quarter note** gets one **beat**. Place **barlines** after every four **beats**.

LESSON 6 *Time Signature*
REVIEW

The last **note** is missing in each **measure**. Write one **note** in each box to complete each **measure**. Put the **note** on any **line** or in any **space**. (Remember, the **time signature** will tell you how many **beats** are in each **measure**, and what **note** gets a **beat**.)

Write one **rest** in each box to complete each **measure**.

On the **staff** below, one **measure** has too many **beats**. Circle the **measure** with too many **beats**.

On the **staff** below, one **measure** doesn't have enough **beats**. Circle that **measure**.

Write the correct **time signature** in the box for each of the following examples.

LESSON 7 *Dots*
REVIEW

MusicMath ✏️

Write the correct **note** in each blank space.

Fill in the correct **dotted note** in the box.

Fill in the correct **dotted rest** in the box.

Place **barlines** in the correct places on this **staff**.

In the **staff** below, circle the **measure** which has too many **beats**.

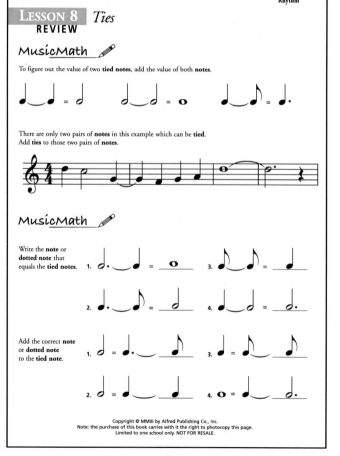

LESSON 8 *Ties*
REVIEW

MusicMath ✏️

To figure out the value of two **tied notes**, add the value of both **notes**.

There are only two pairs of **notes** in this example which can be **tied**. Add **ties** to those two pairs of **notes**.

MusicMath ✏️

Write the **note** or **dotted note** that equals the **tied notes**.

Add the correct **note** or **dotted note** to the **tied note**.

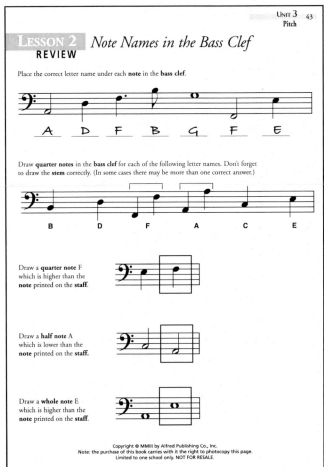

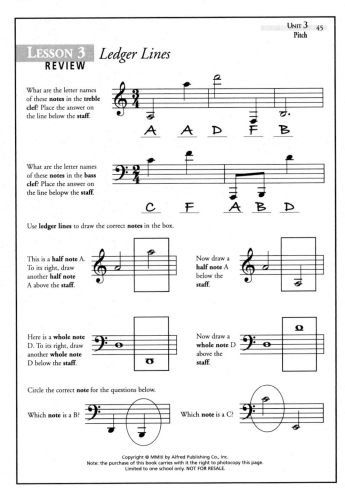

LESSON 6 *Key Signatures*
REVIEW

Look at the musical examples on the left. These examples have **sharps** or **flats** but no **key signature**. In the **staff** on the right, draw the same **notes**, without **sharps** or **flats**, and add the correct **key signature**.

Draw the **key signature** with three **flats**. We've drawn the first **flat** for you.

Draw the **key signature** with three **sharps**. We've drawn the first **sharp** for you.

Below are three pairs of **key signatures**. In each pair, one is drawn correctly and one is drawn incorrectly. Circle the correct **key signature** in each pair.

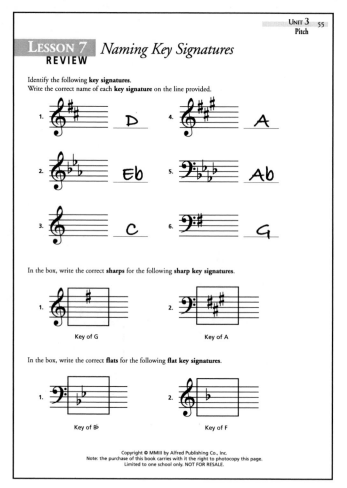

LESSON 7 *Naming Key Signatures*
REVIEW

Identify the following **key signatures**.
Write the correct name of each **key signature** on the line provided.

1. D   4. A
2. Eb   5. Ab
3. C   6. G

In the box, write the correct **sharps** for the following **sharp key signatures**.

1. Key of G   2. Key of A

In the box, write the correct **flats** for the following **flat key signatures**.

1. Key of Bb   2. Key of F

LESSON 8 *Natural Sign and Accidentals*
REVIEW

What **note** is in the box? Circle the correct answer.

1. F or (F#)
2. Bb or (B)
3. (G) or G#
4. (A♮) or Ab

Using **half notes**, draw the following **notes** in the **treble clef**. There will be more than one correct answer.

Bb   D#   Eb   E♮   Ab

Using **quarter notes**, draw the following **notes** in the **bass clef**. There will be more than one correct answer.

G#   C#   F♮   C♮   Ab

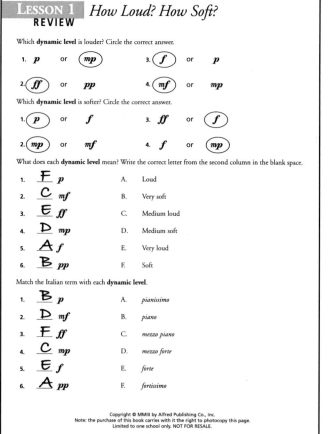

LESSON 1 *How Loud? How Soft?*
REVIEW

Which **dynamic level** is louder? Circle the correct answer.

1. *p* or (*mp*)   3. (*f*) or *p*
2. (*ff*) or *pp*   4. (*mf*) or *mp*

Which **dynamic level** is softer? Circle the correct answer.

1. (*p*) or *f*   3. *ff* or (*f*)
2. (*mp*) or *mf*   4. *f* or (*mp*)

What does each **dynamic level** mean? Write the correct letter from the second column in the blank space.

1. F *p*   A. Loud
2. C *mf*   B. Very soft
3. E *ff*   C. Medium loud
4. D *mp*   D. Medium soft
5. A *f*   E. Very loud
6. B *pp*   F. Soft

Match the Italian term with each **dynamic level**.

1. B *p*   A. *pianissimo*
2. D *mf*   B. *piano*
3. F *ff*   C. *mezzo piano*
4. C *mp*   D. *mezzo forte*
5. E *f*   E. *forte*
6. A *pp*   F. *fortissimo*

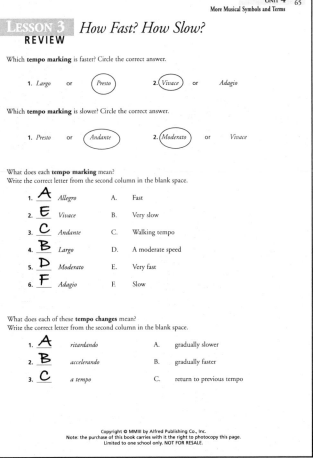

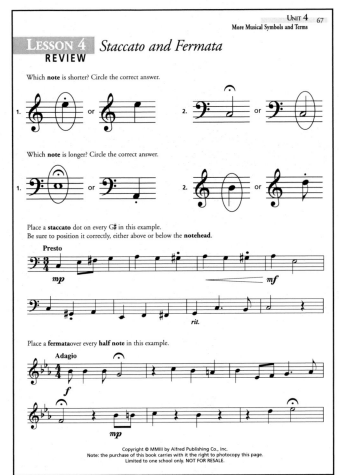

A Performance Piece

The Water is Wide

American Folk Song
Arranged by **JAY ALTHOUSE**

Certificate of Completion

_____
(name of student)

has completed the lessons in the book *Ready to Read Music*, can identify the symbols of music, and, therefore, is now

READY TO READ MUSIC

_____
Teacher

Jay Althouse, *Author*